The Cotswolds
Colouring Book

First published 2017
Reprinted 2019

The History Press
The Mill, Brimscombe Port
Stroud, Gloucestershire, GL5 2QG
www.thehistorypress.co.uk

Text © The History Press, 2017
Illustrations by Martin Latham © The History Press, 2017

The right of The History Press to be identified as the Author of this work has been asserted in accordance with the Copyright, Designs and Patents Act 1988.

All rights reserved. No part of this book may be reprinted or reproduced or utilised in any form or by any electronic, mechanical or other means, now known or hereafter invented, including photocopying and recording, or in any information storage or retrieval system, without the permission in writing from the Publishers.

British Library Cataloguing in Publication Data.
A catalogue record for this book is available from the British Library.

ISBN 978 0 7509 7999 3

Typesetting and origination by The History Press
Printed and bound by Imak, Turkey.

THE COTSWOLDS
COLOURING BOOK

PAST AND PRESENT

Take some time out of your busy life to relax and unwind with this feel-good colouring book designed for everyone who loves the Cotswolds.

Absorb yourself in the simple action of colouring in the scenes and settings from around the region, past and present. From rolling hills and honey-coloured villages, to thatched cottages and majestic country houses, you are sure to find some of your favourite locations waiting to be transformed with a splash of colour.

There are no rules – choose any page and any choice of colouring pens or pencils you like to create your own unique, colourful and creative illustrations.

Bibury, Gloucestershire ▸

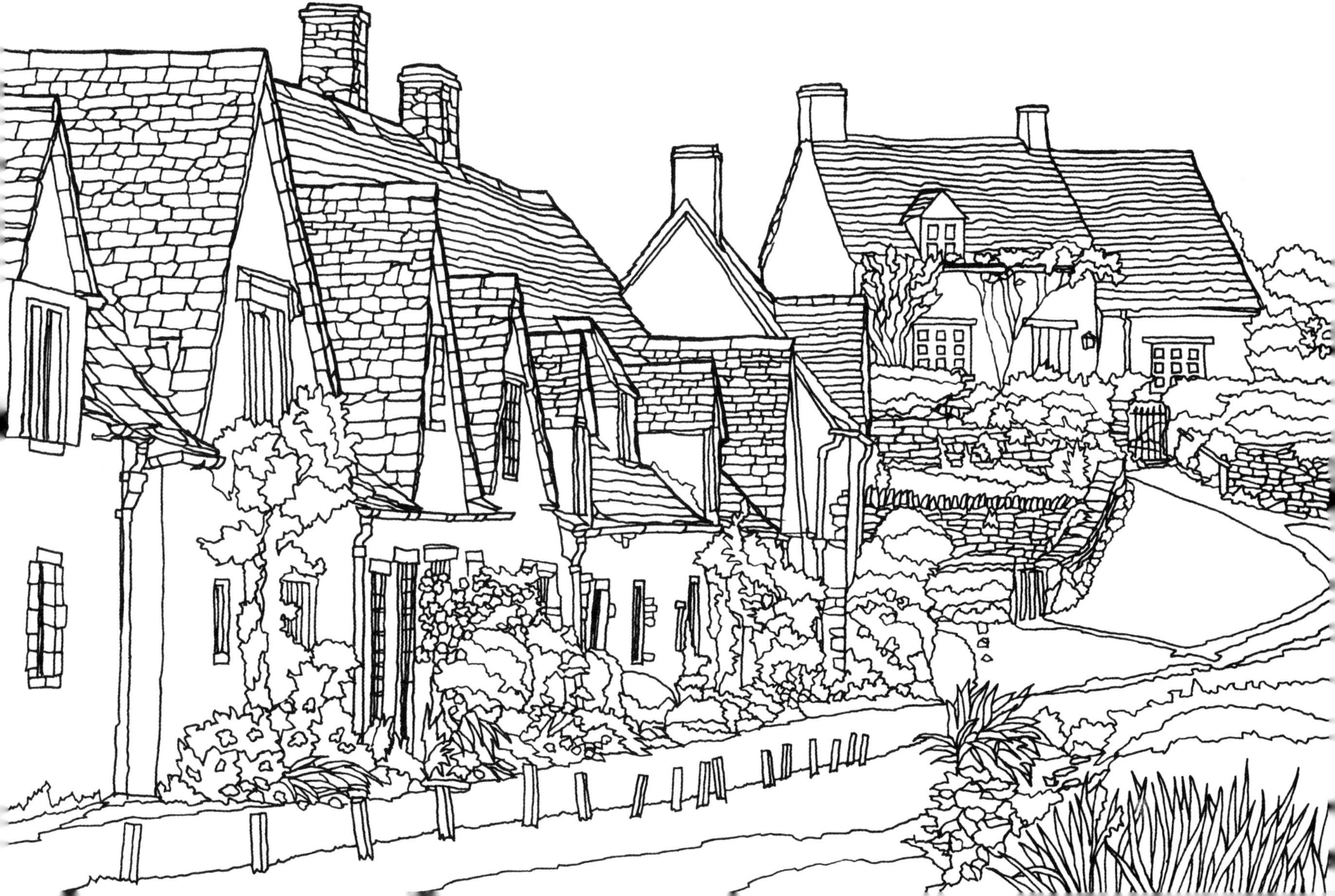

A view of Nailsworth, Gloucestershire ▶

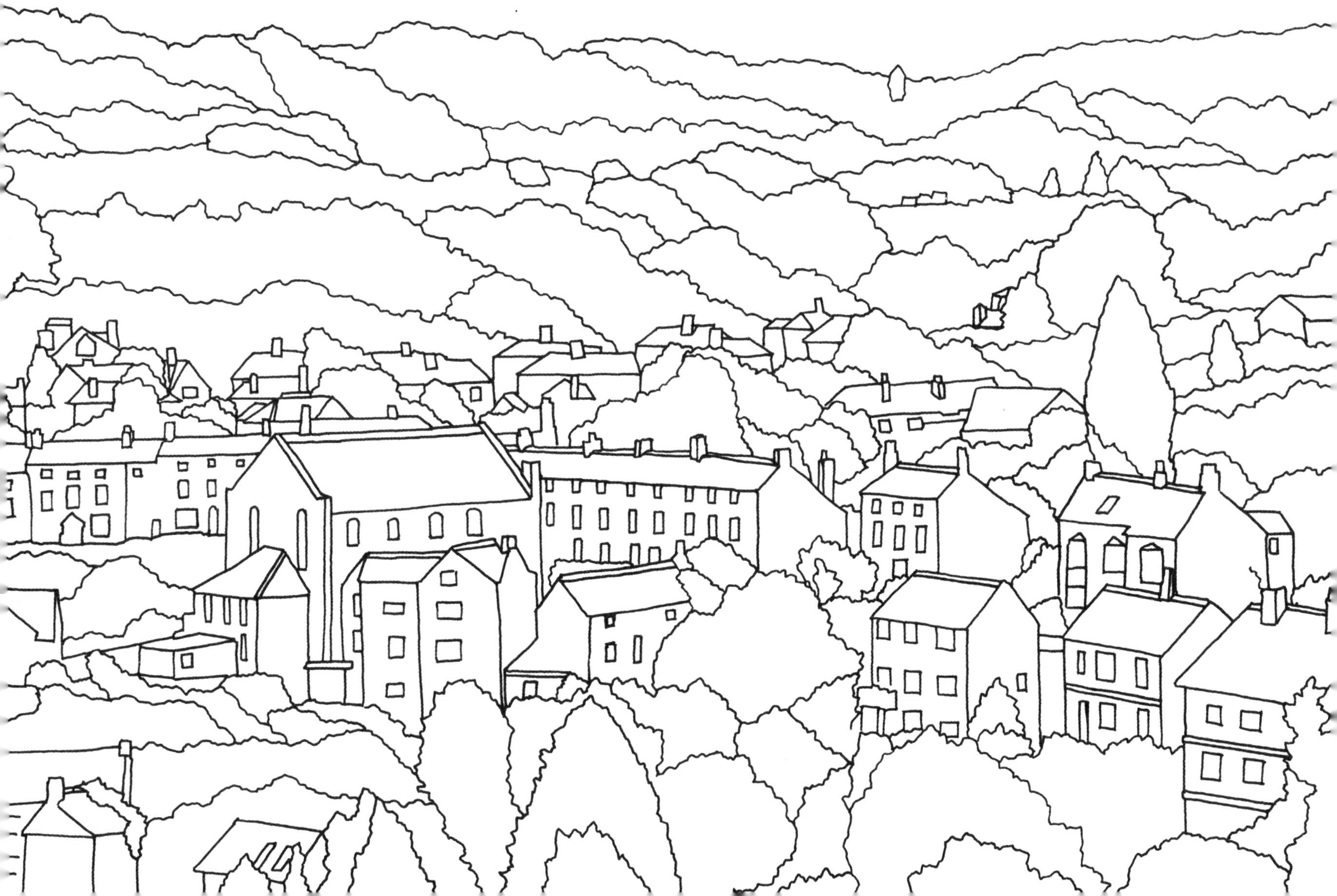

Berkeley Castle, Gloucestershire ▸

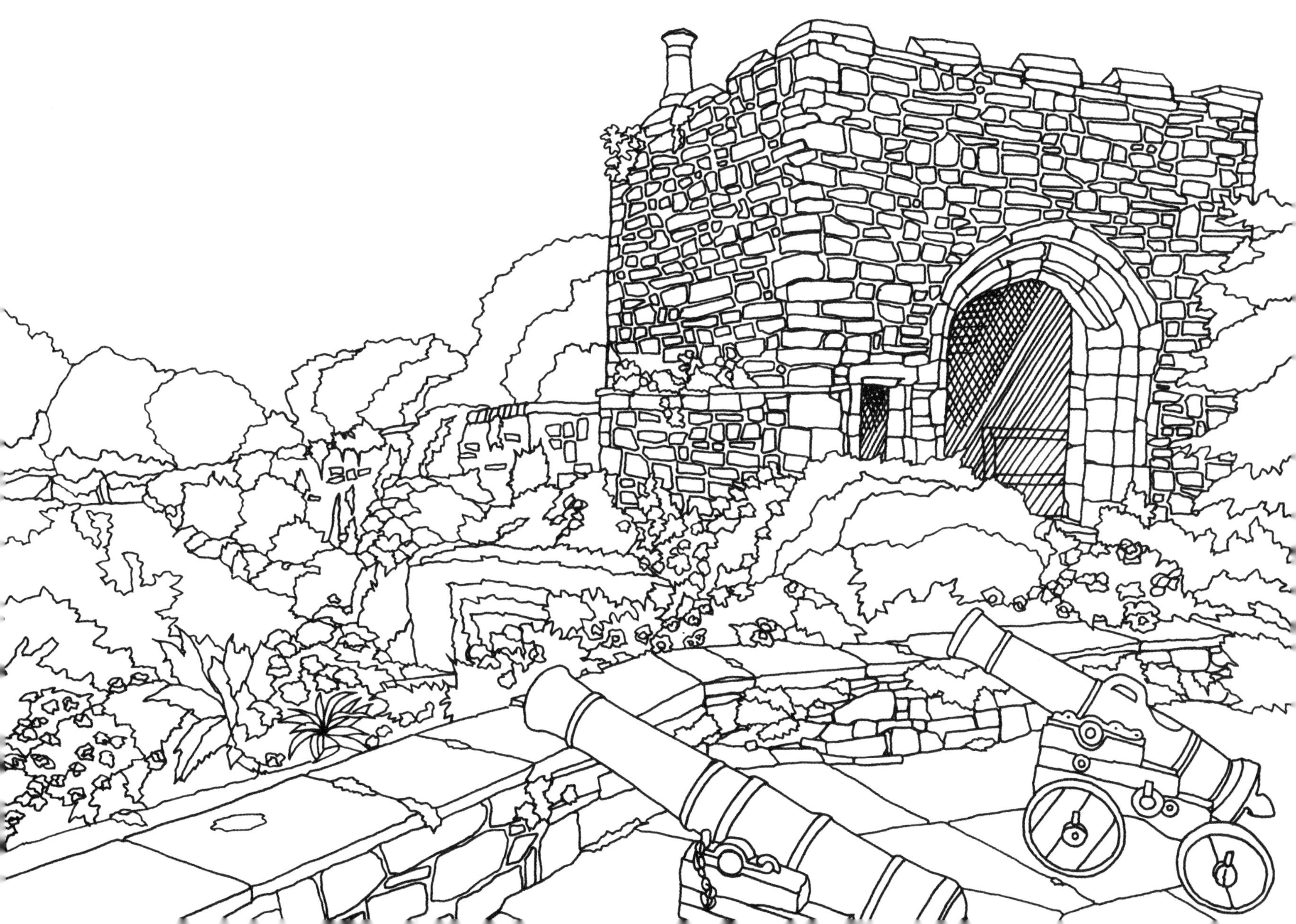

Blenheim Palace, Oxfordshire ▸

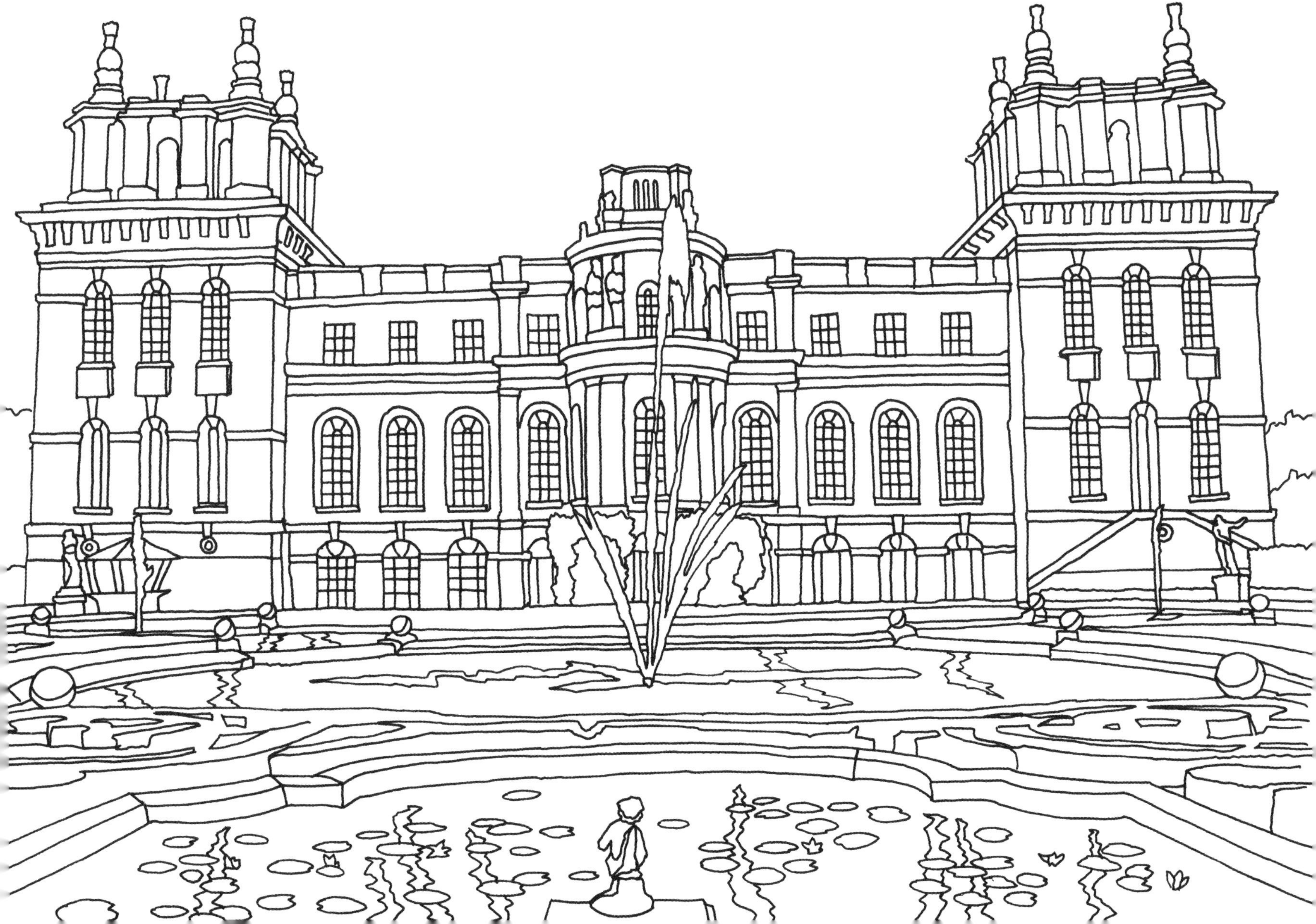

Broadway Tower, Worcestershire ▶

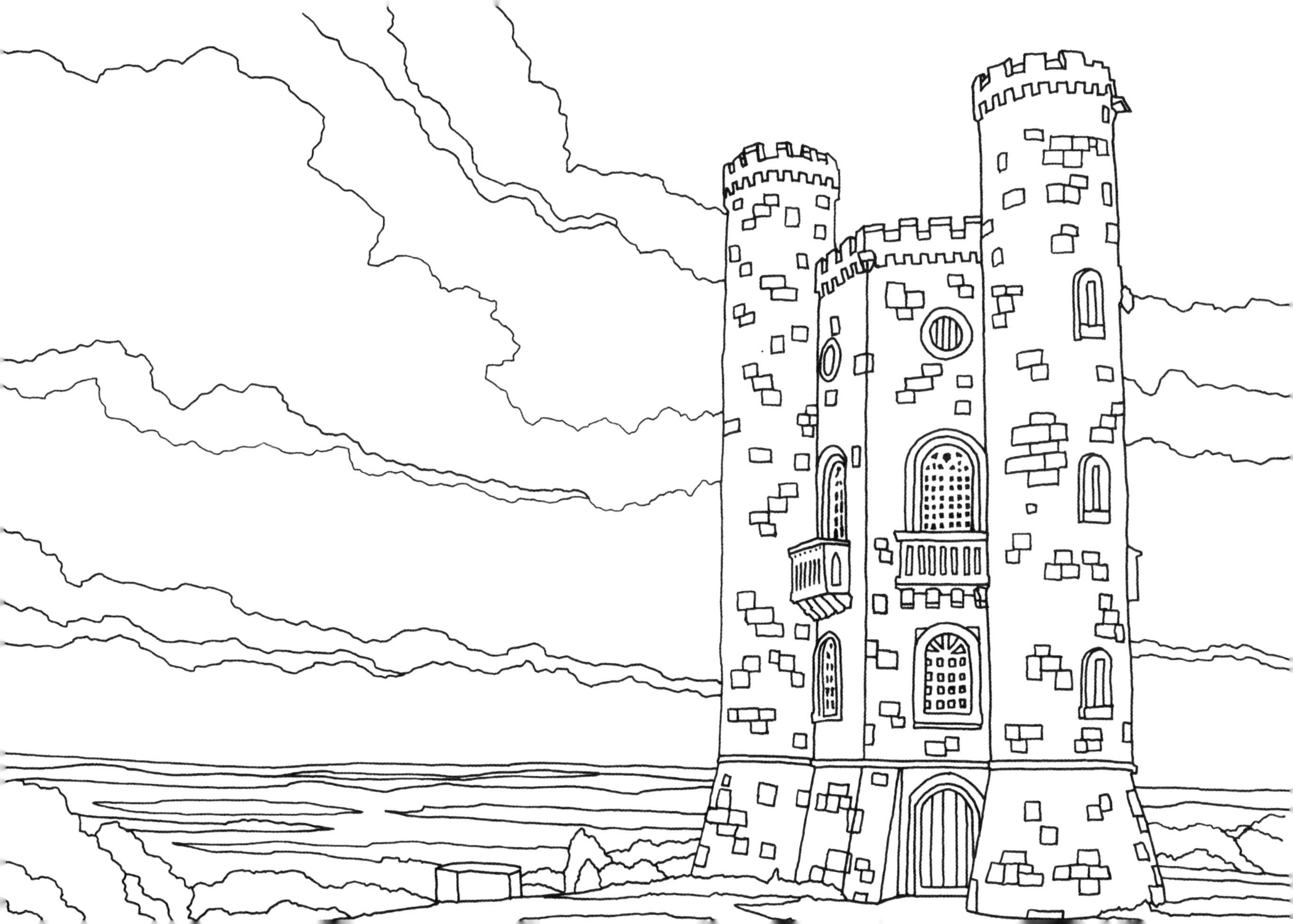

Bourton-on-the-Water, Gloucestershire ▶

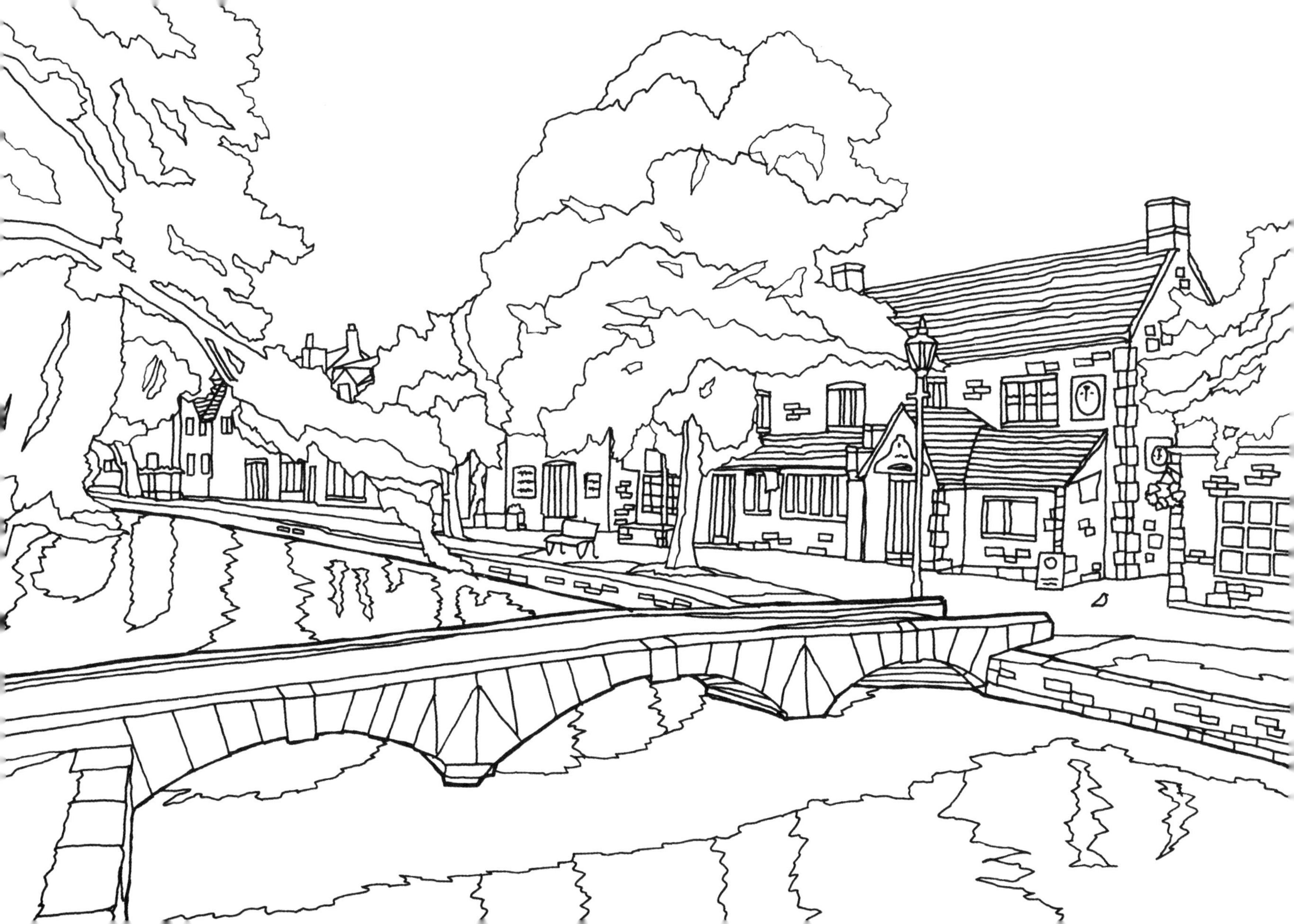

Saker Falcons at the Cotswold Falconry Centre, Gloucestershire ▸

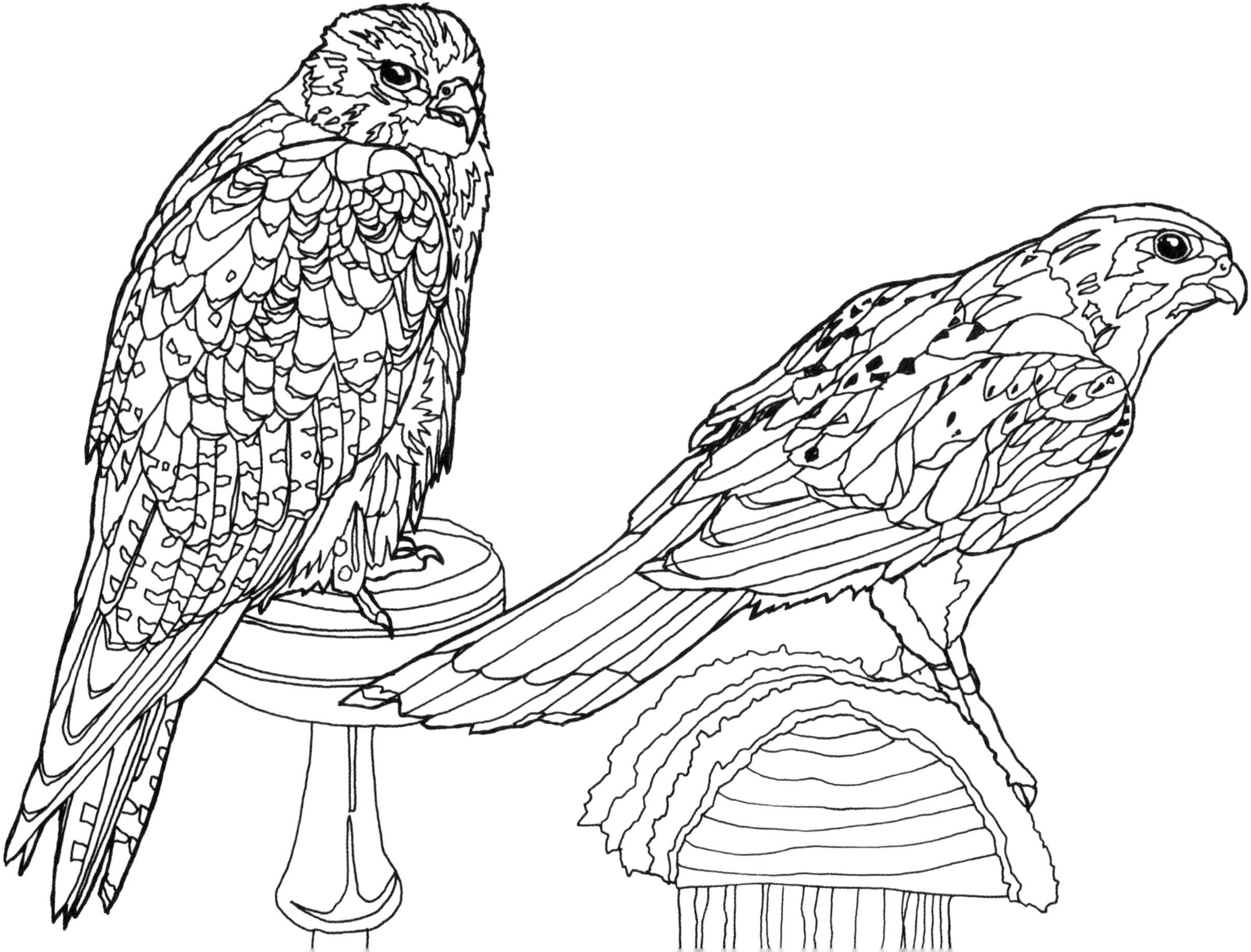

Burford, Oxfordshire ▸

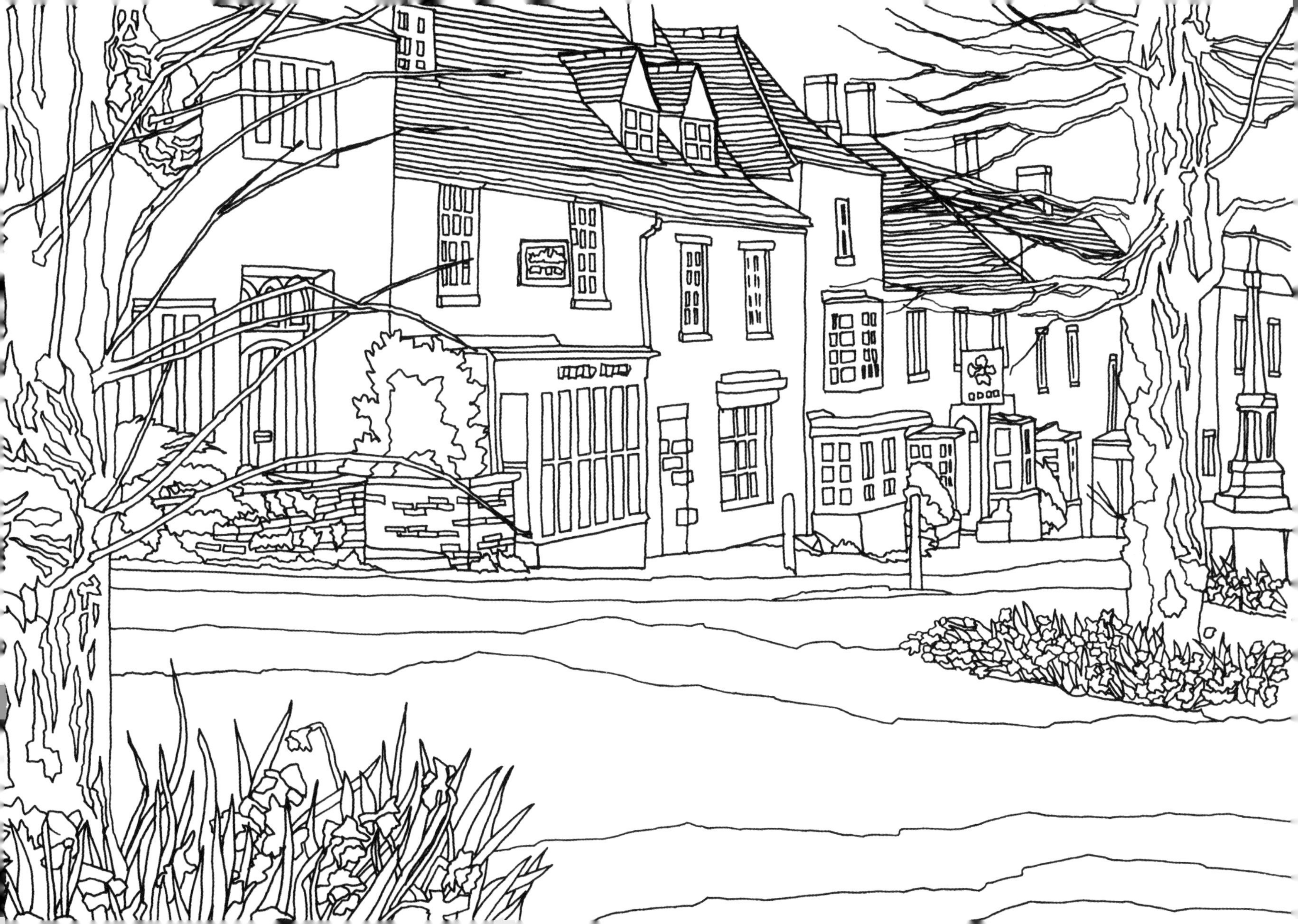

Chastleton House, Oxfordshire ▸

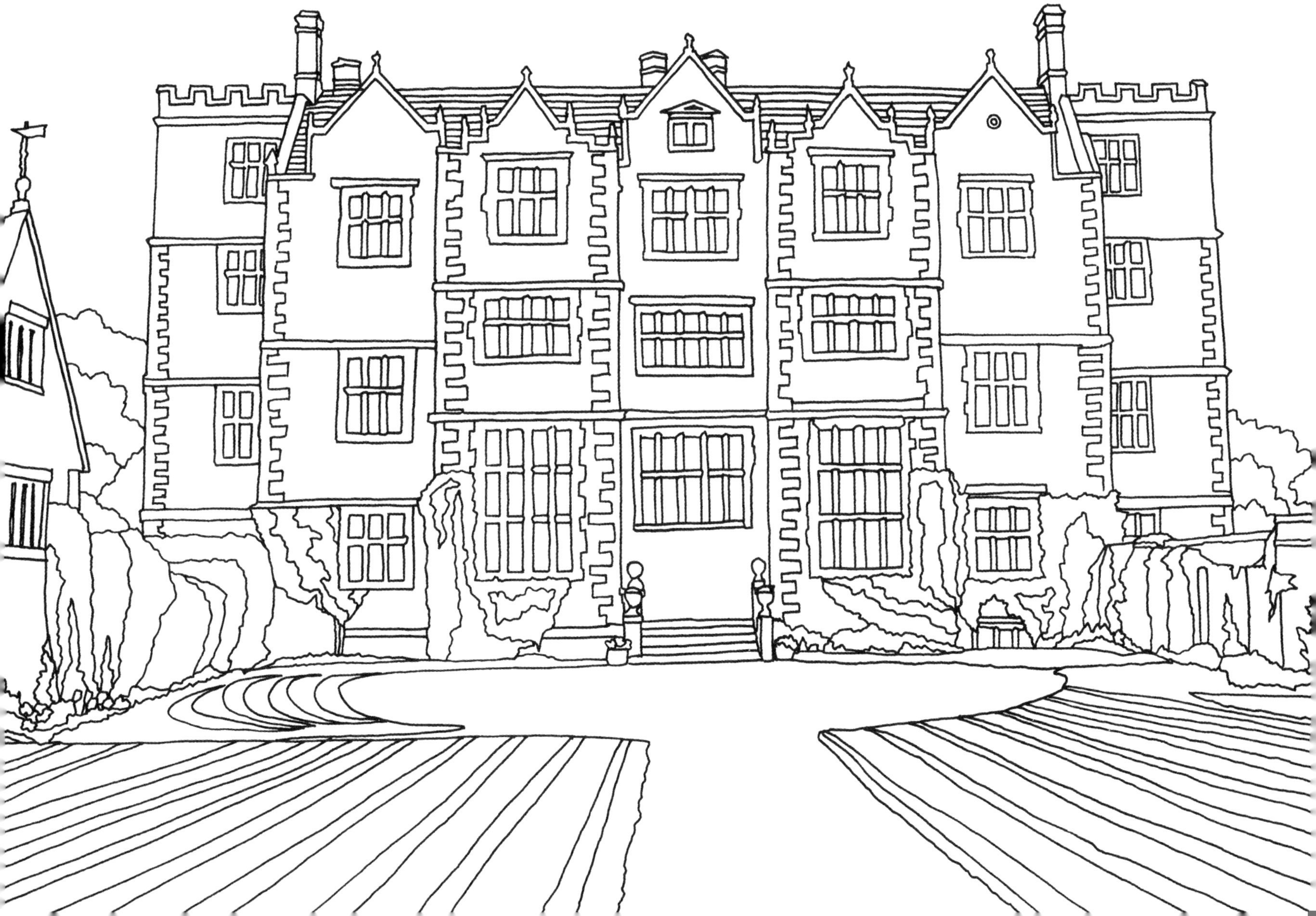

Cheese Rolling at Cooper's Hill, Gloucestershire ▸

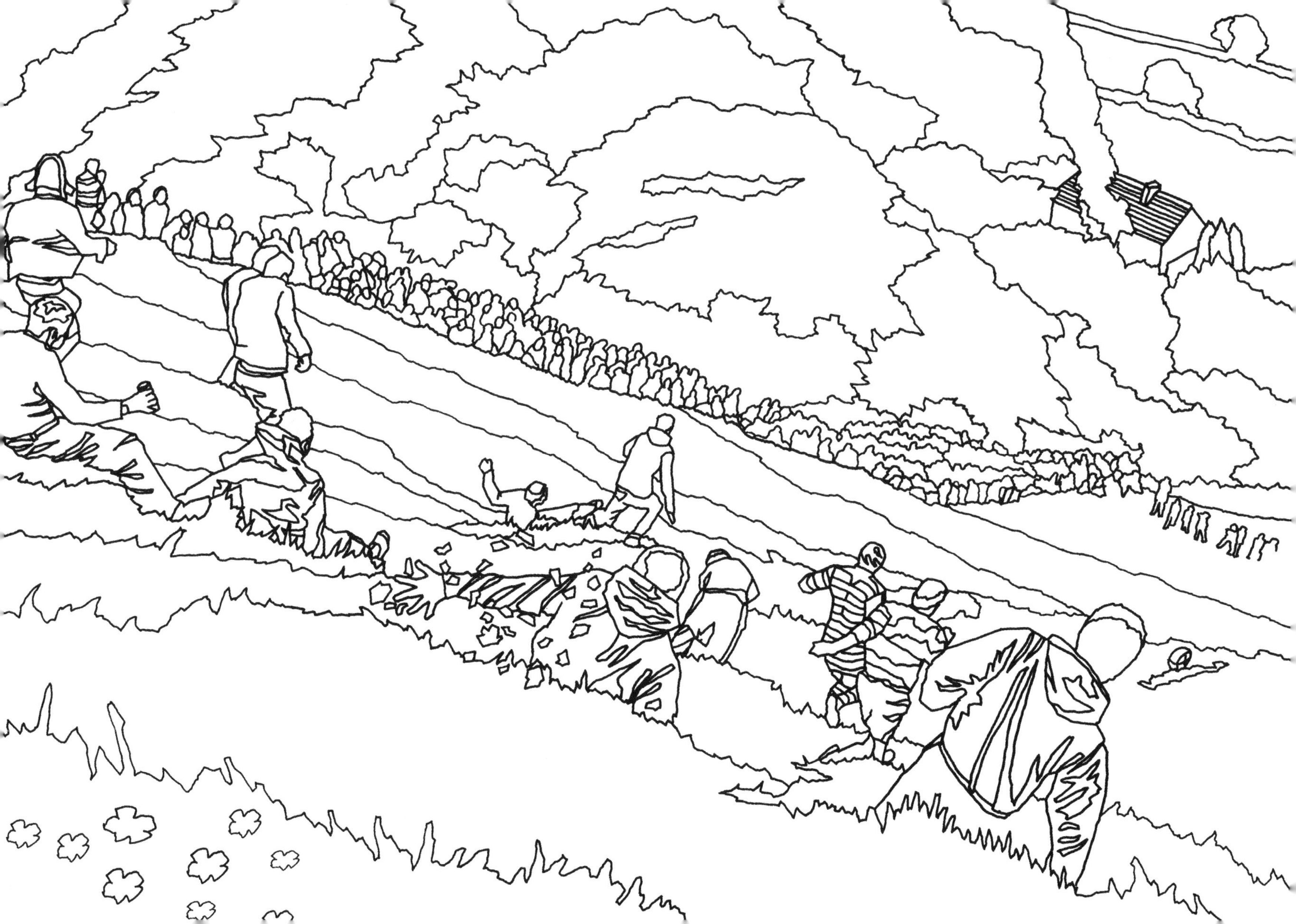

Broadway, Worcestershire ▶

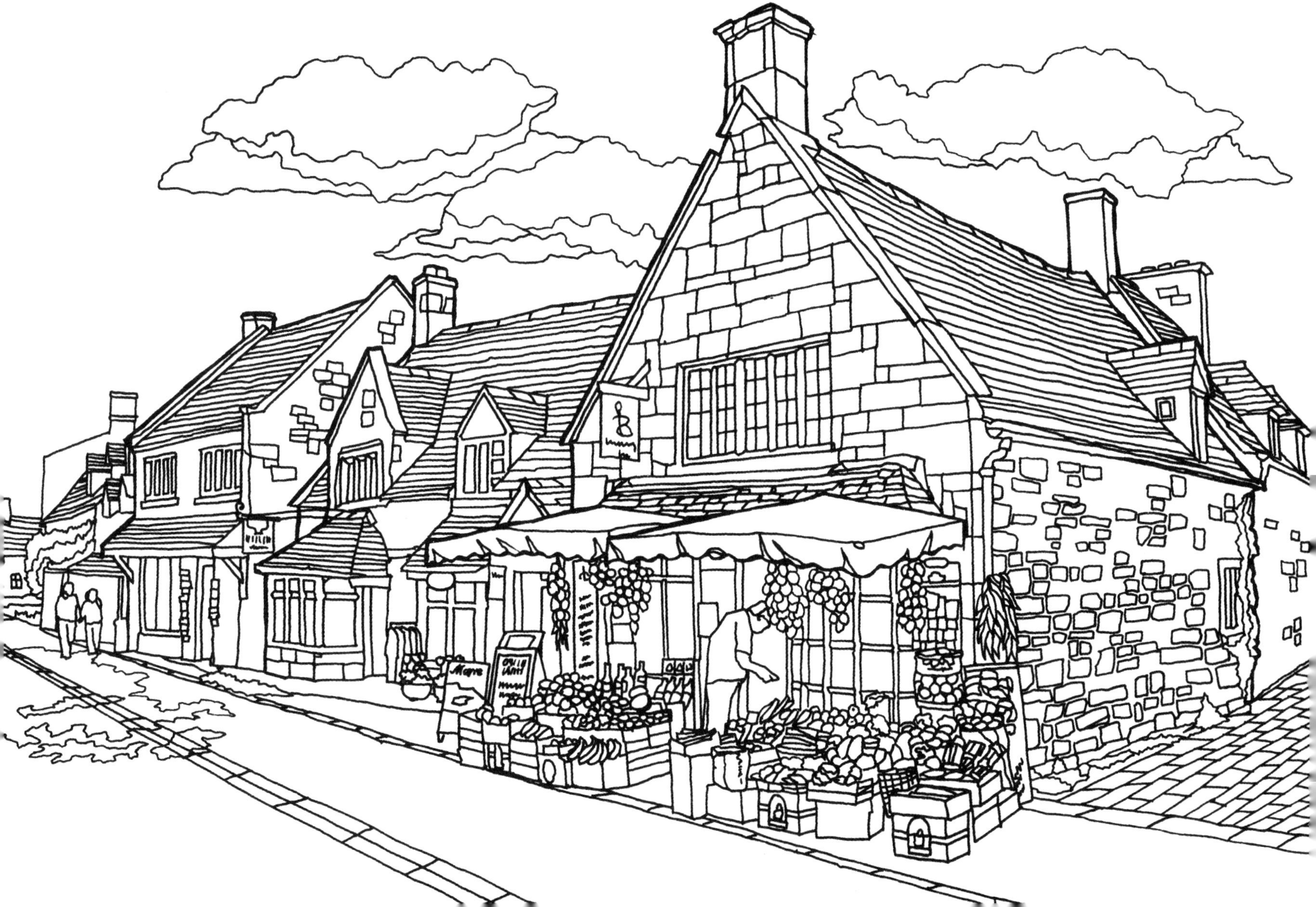

Cheltenham Town Hall, Gloucestershire ▸

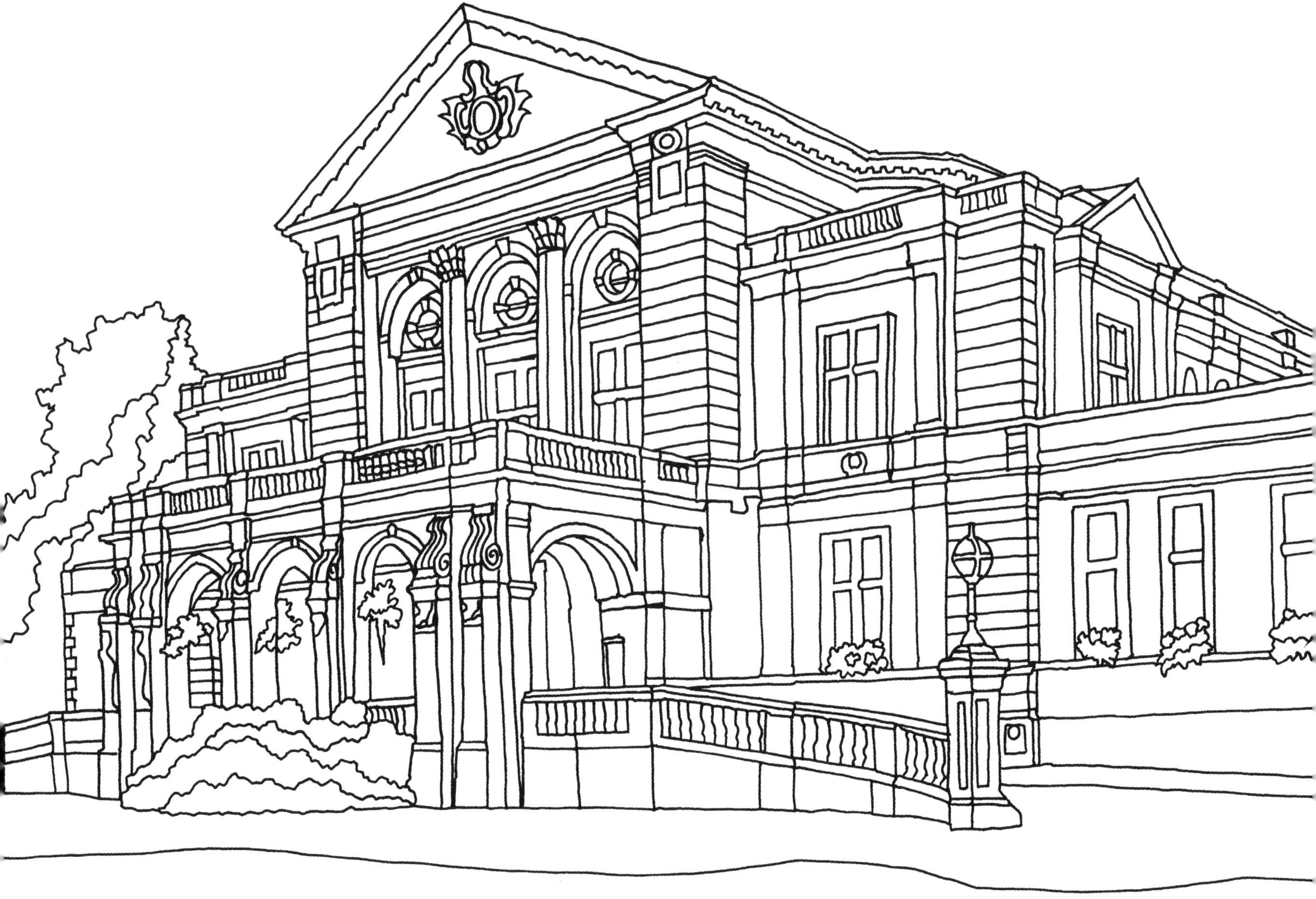

Cheltenham Racecourse, Gloucestershire ▶

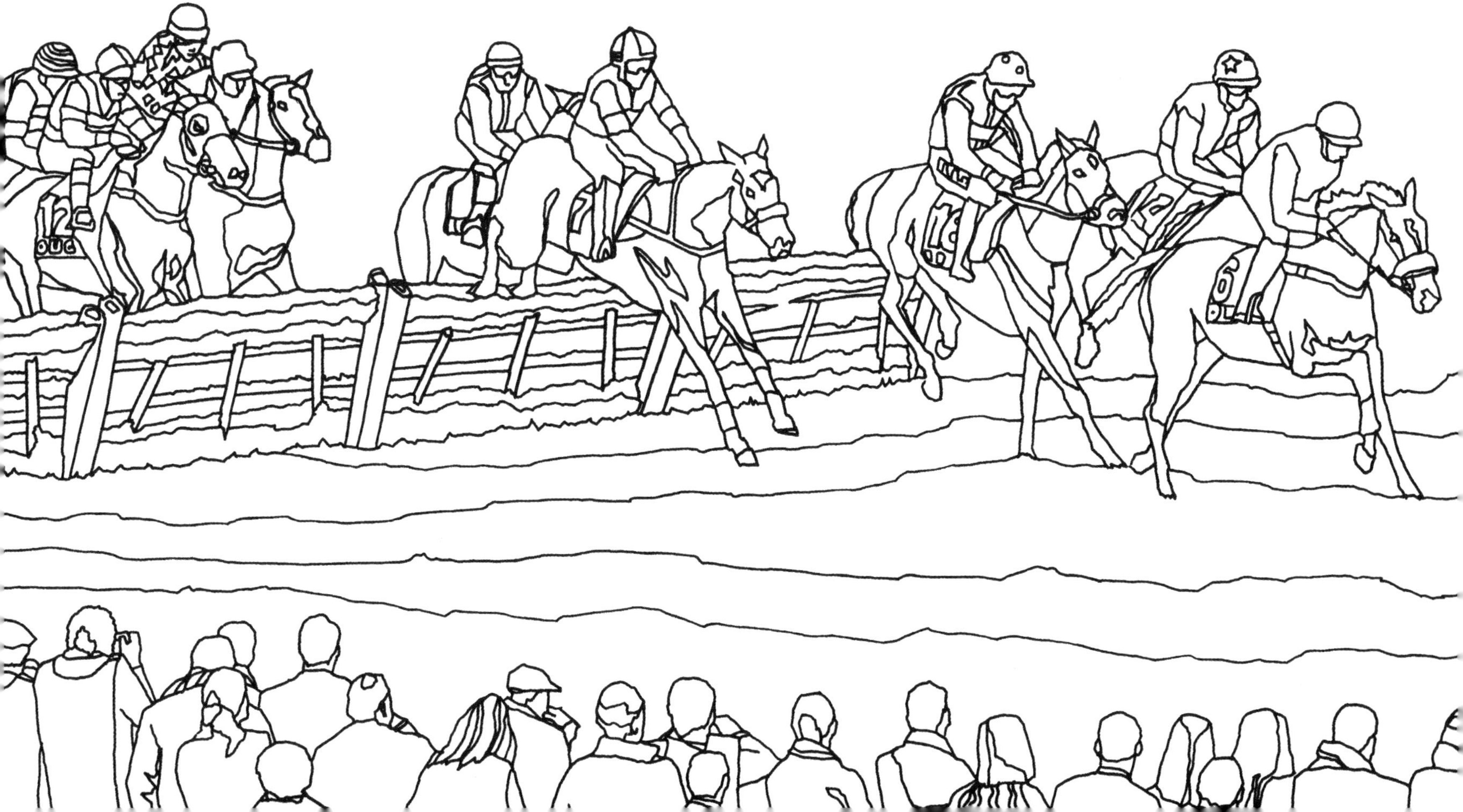
12
7
18
6

Chipping Norton and Bliss Mill, Oxfordshire ▸

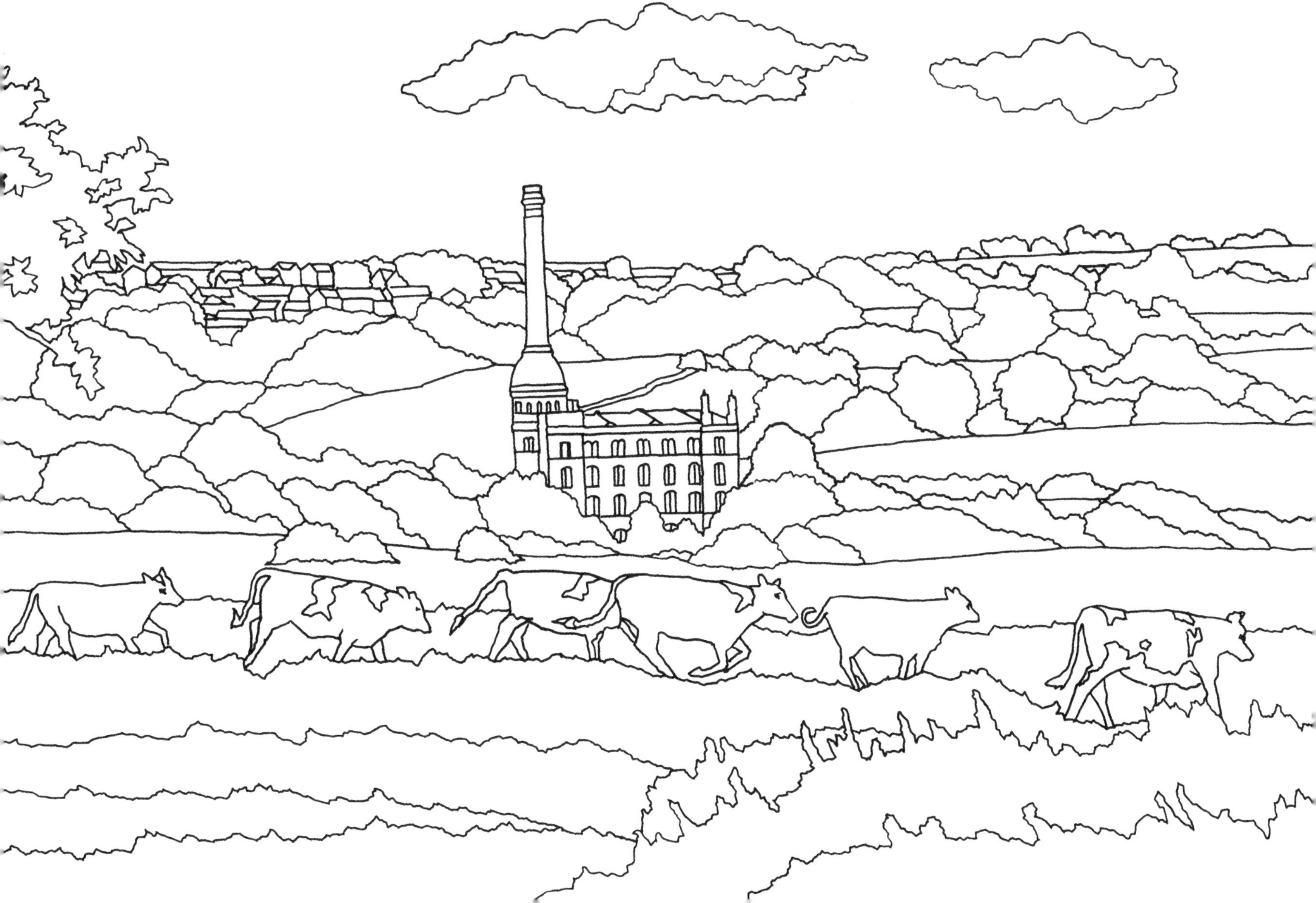

Chipping Steps, Tetbury, Gloucestershire ▸

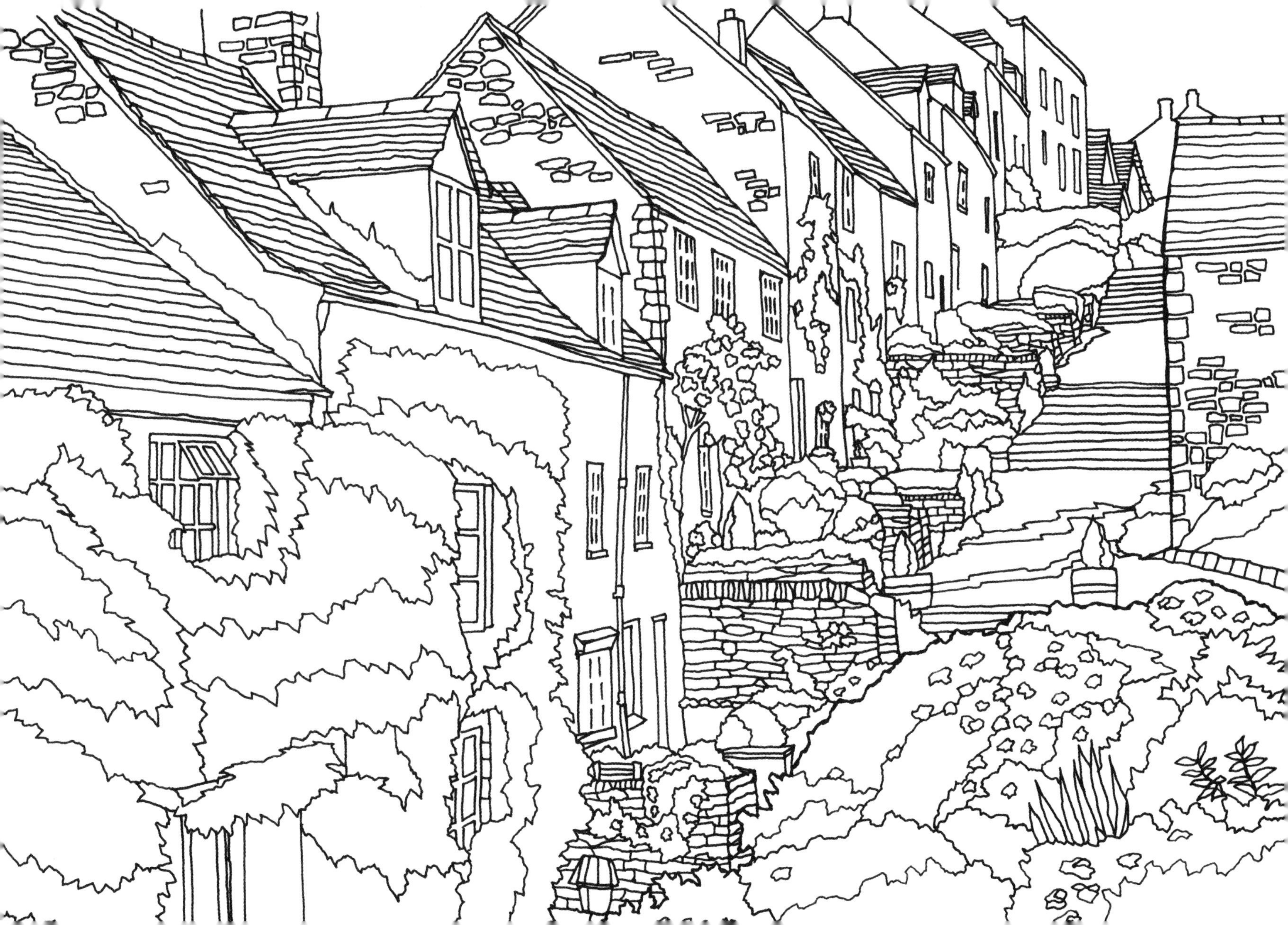

Cirencester market place, Gloucestershire ▸

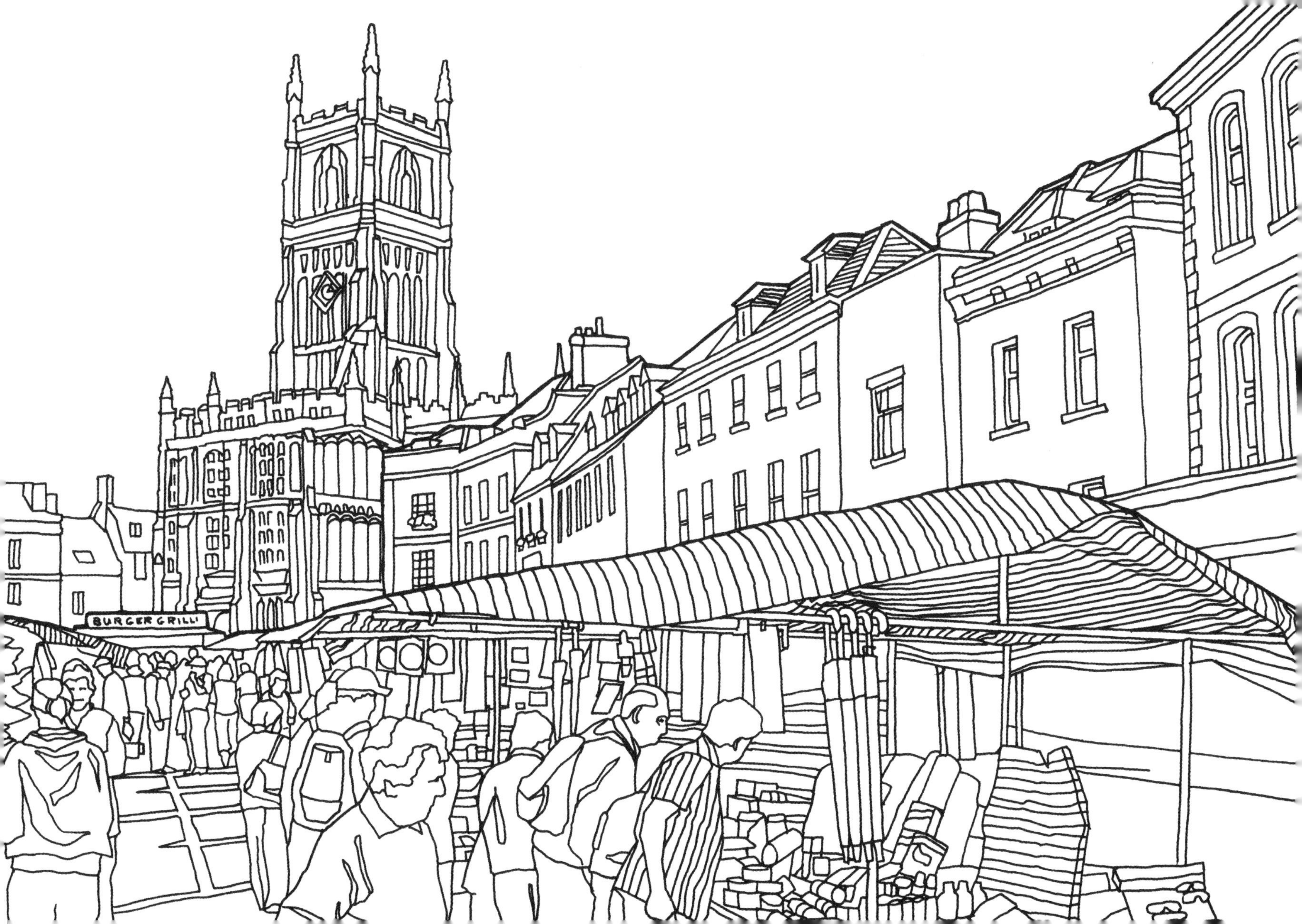
BURGER GRILL

Cogges Manor Farm, Oxfordshire ▸

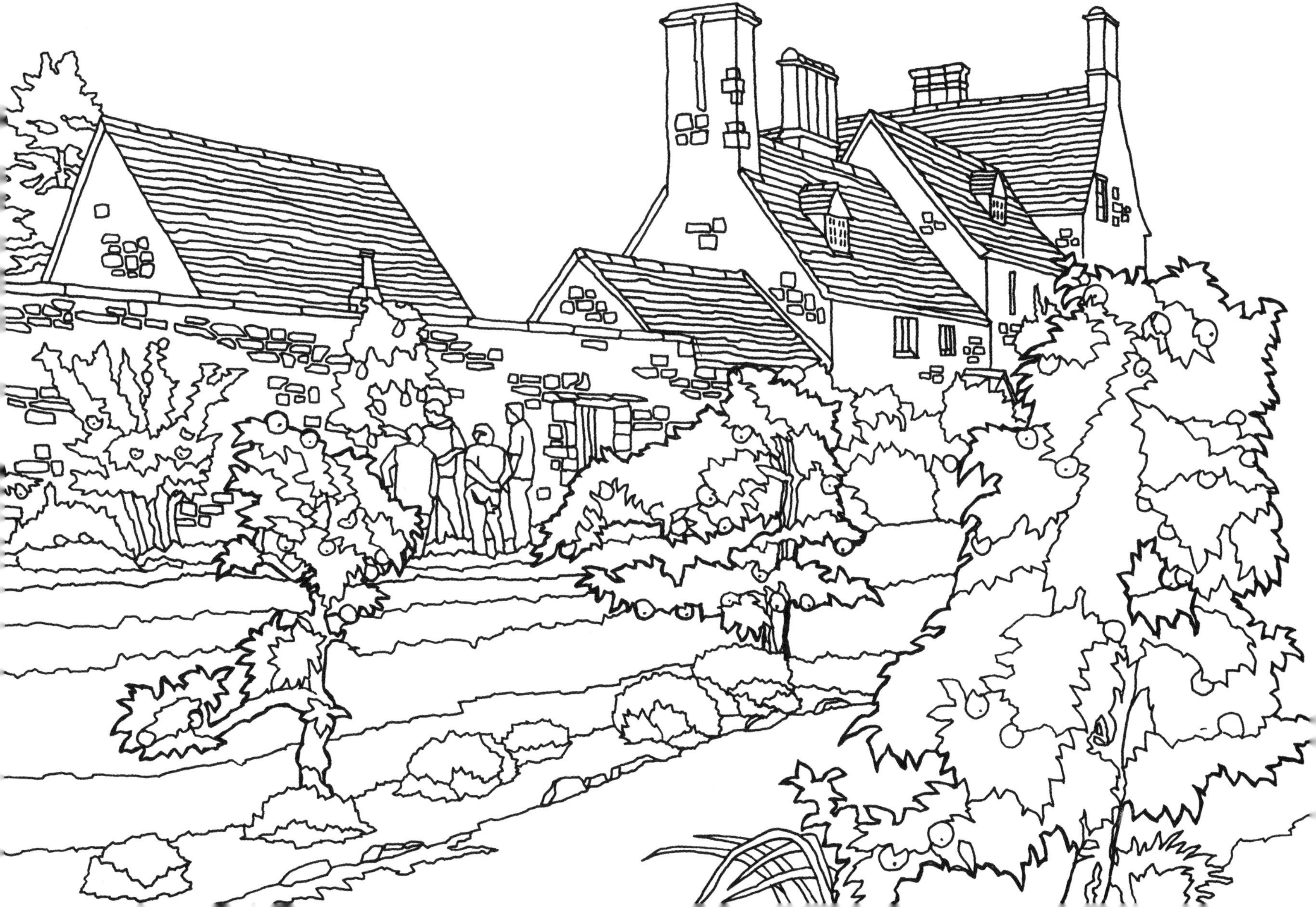

Cotswold sheep ▶

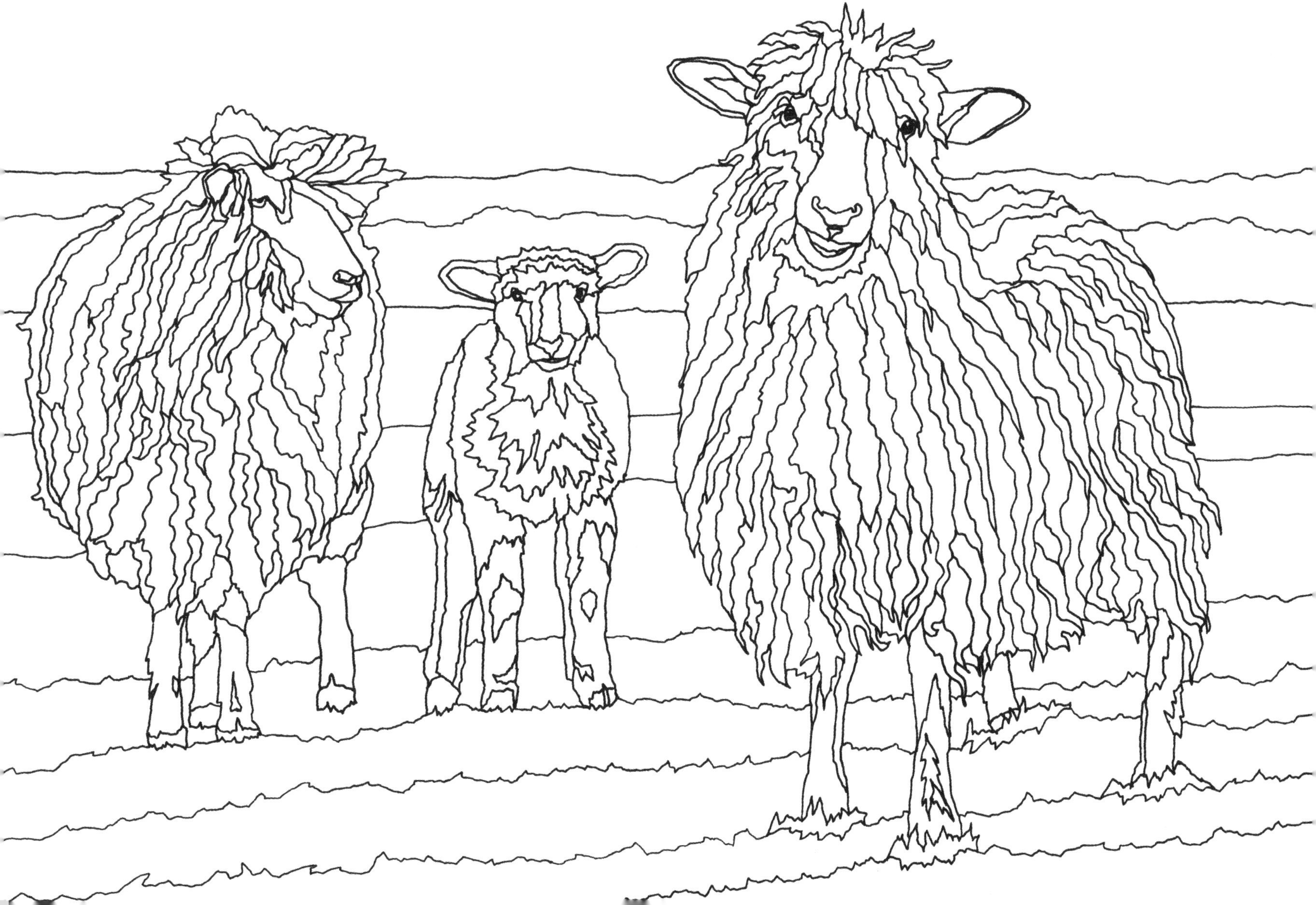

The Dragonfly Maze at Bourton-on-the-Water
in Gloucestershire was designed by Kit Williams ▶

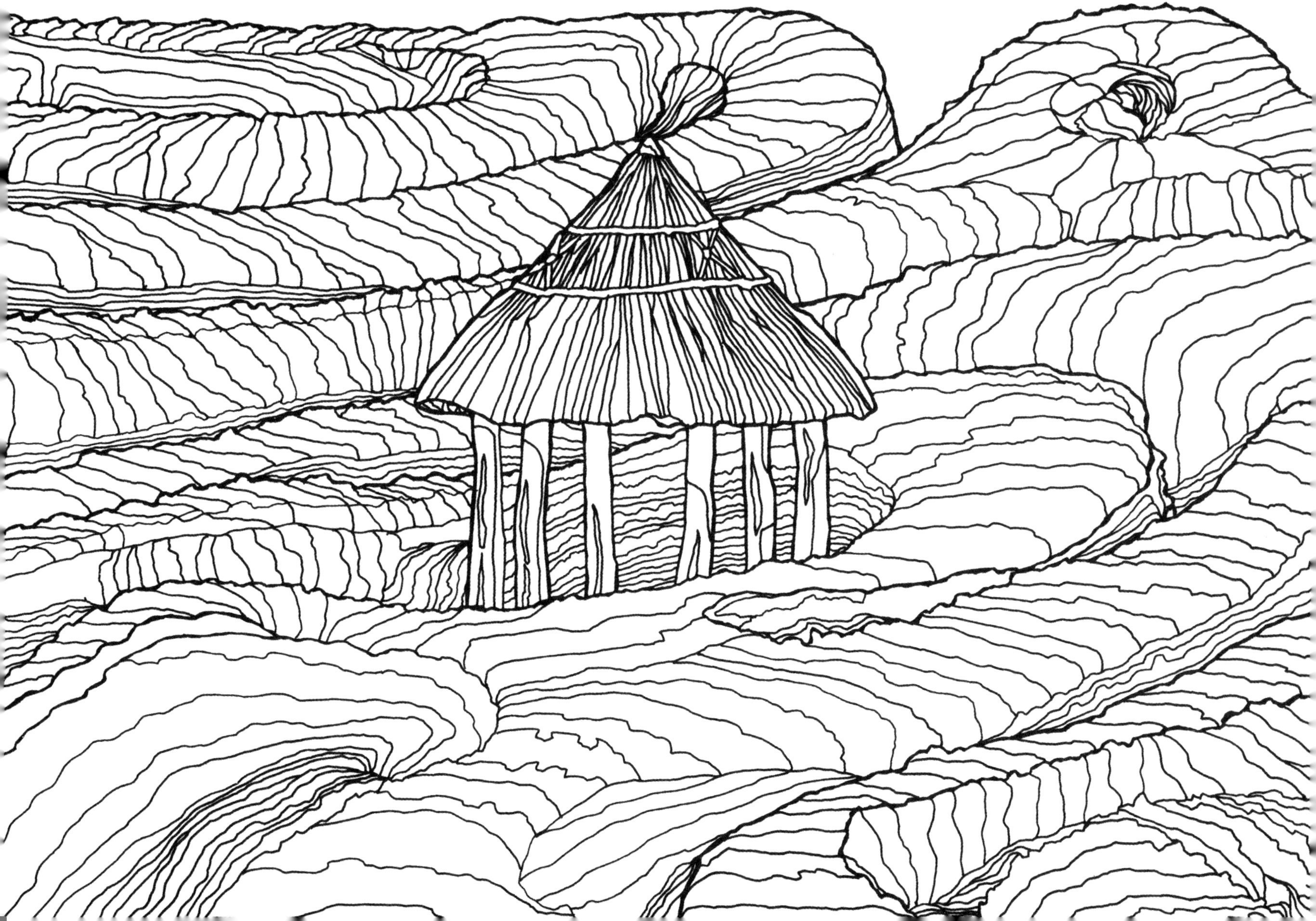

Fairford High Street, Gloucestershire,
at the turn of the century ▶

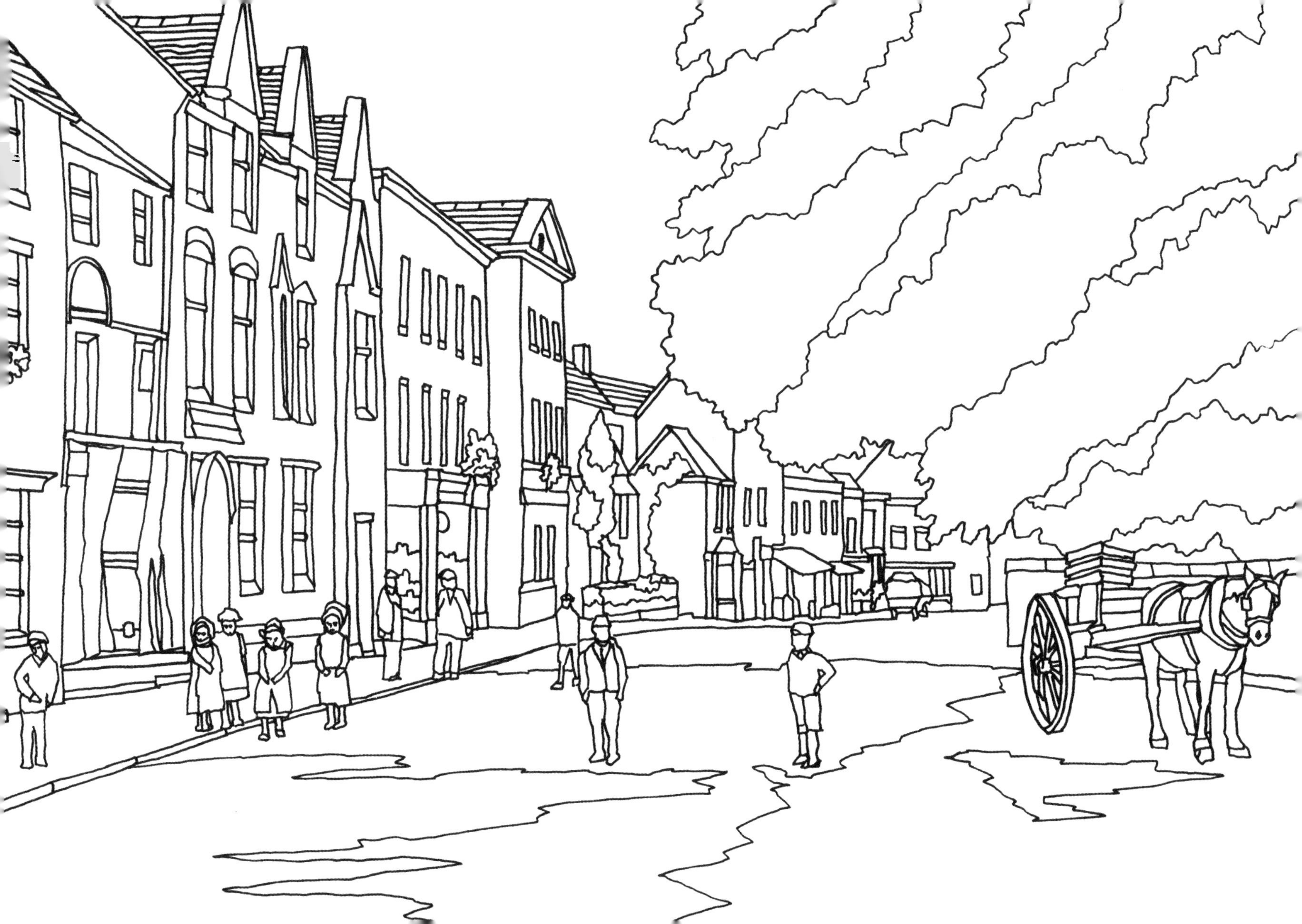

Gloucester Cathedral ▶

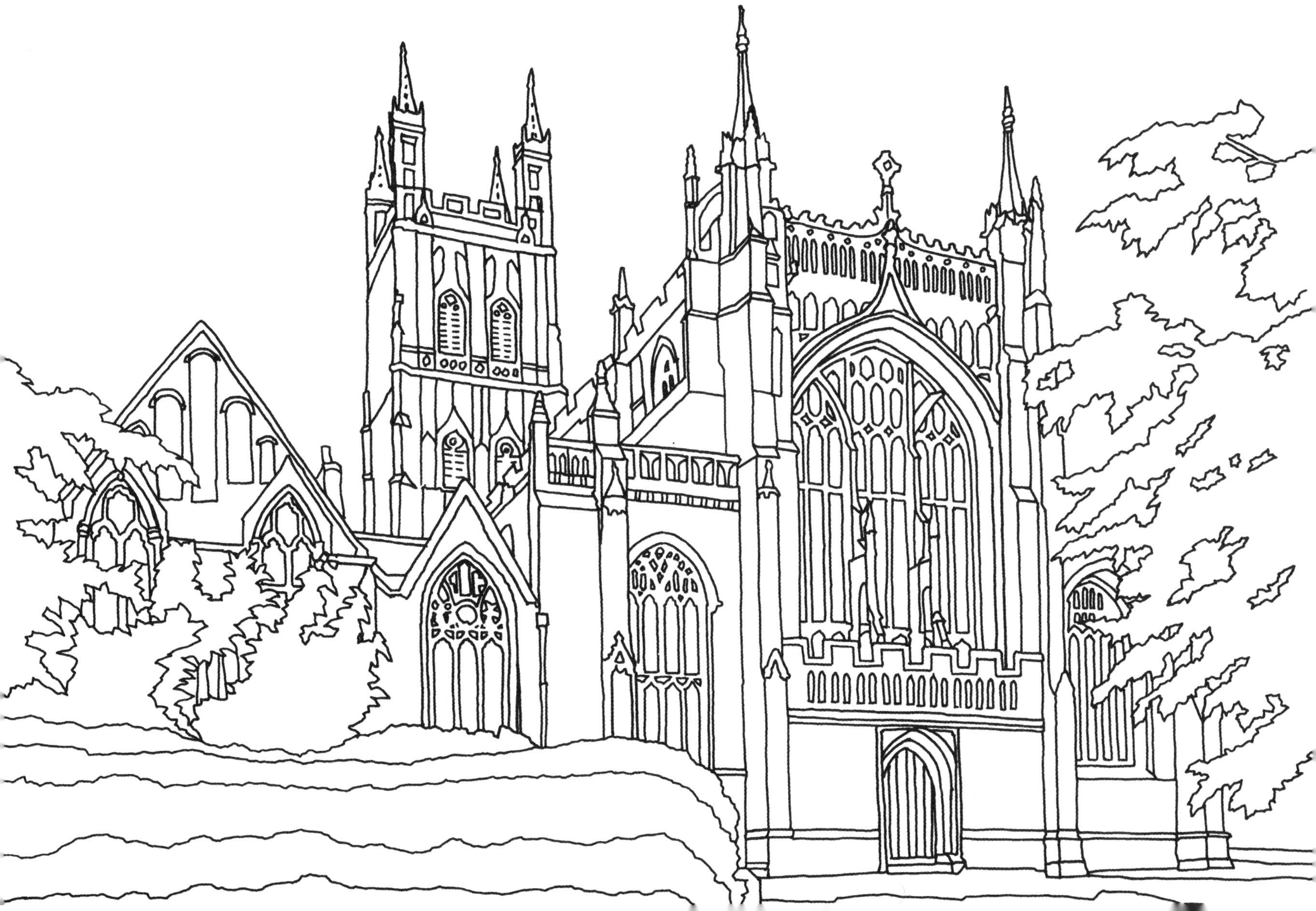

Flamingos at WWT Slimbridge
Wetland Centre, Gloucestershire ▸

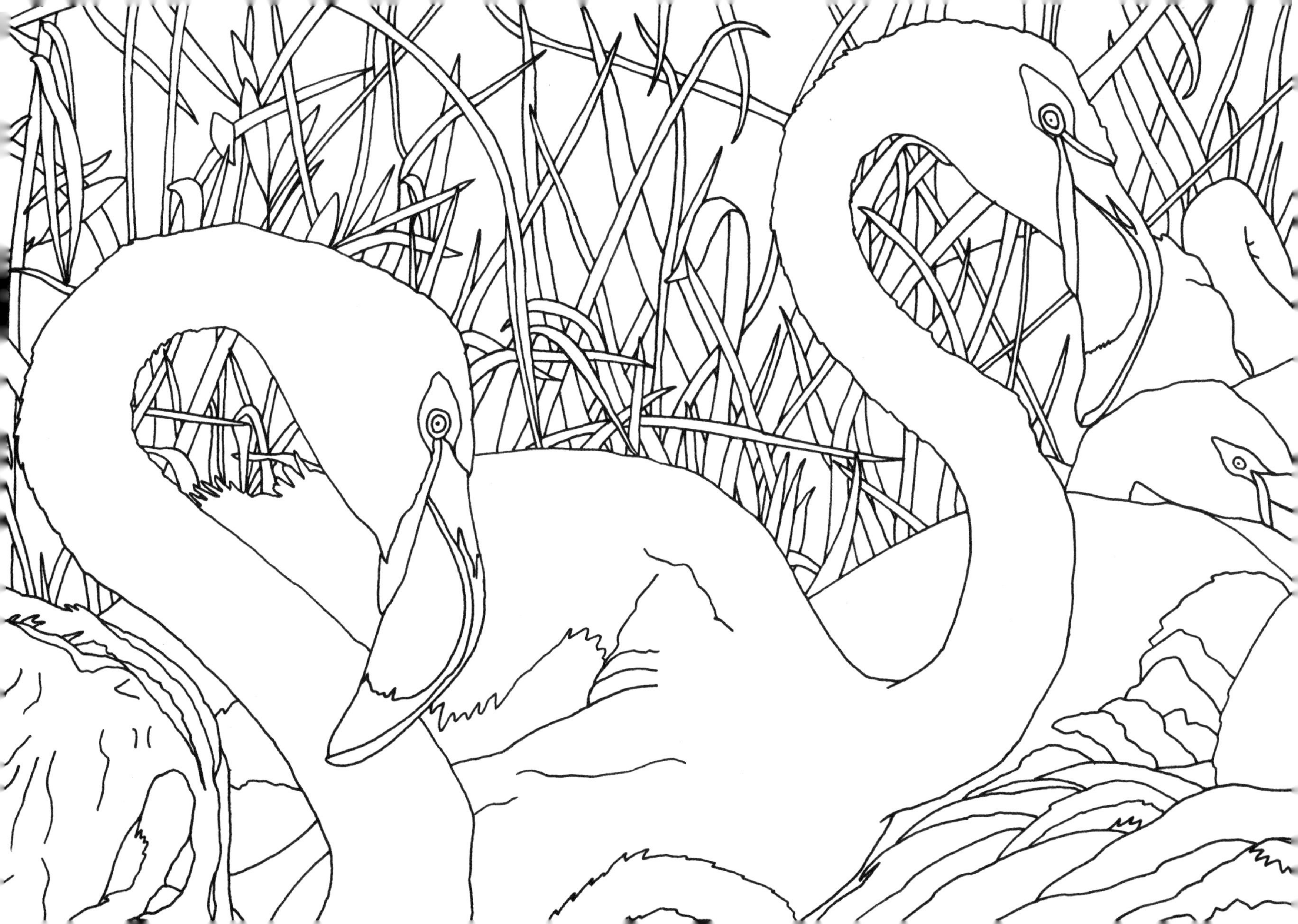

Gloucester Docks, Gloucestershire ▸

ALEXANDRA
WAREHOUSE
ALEXANDRA
WAREHOUSE
HARBOUR HOUSE
BADGER

Hailes Abbey, Gloucestershire ▶

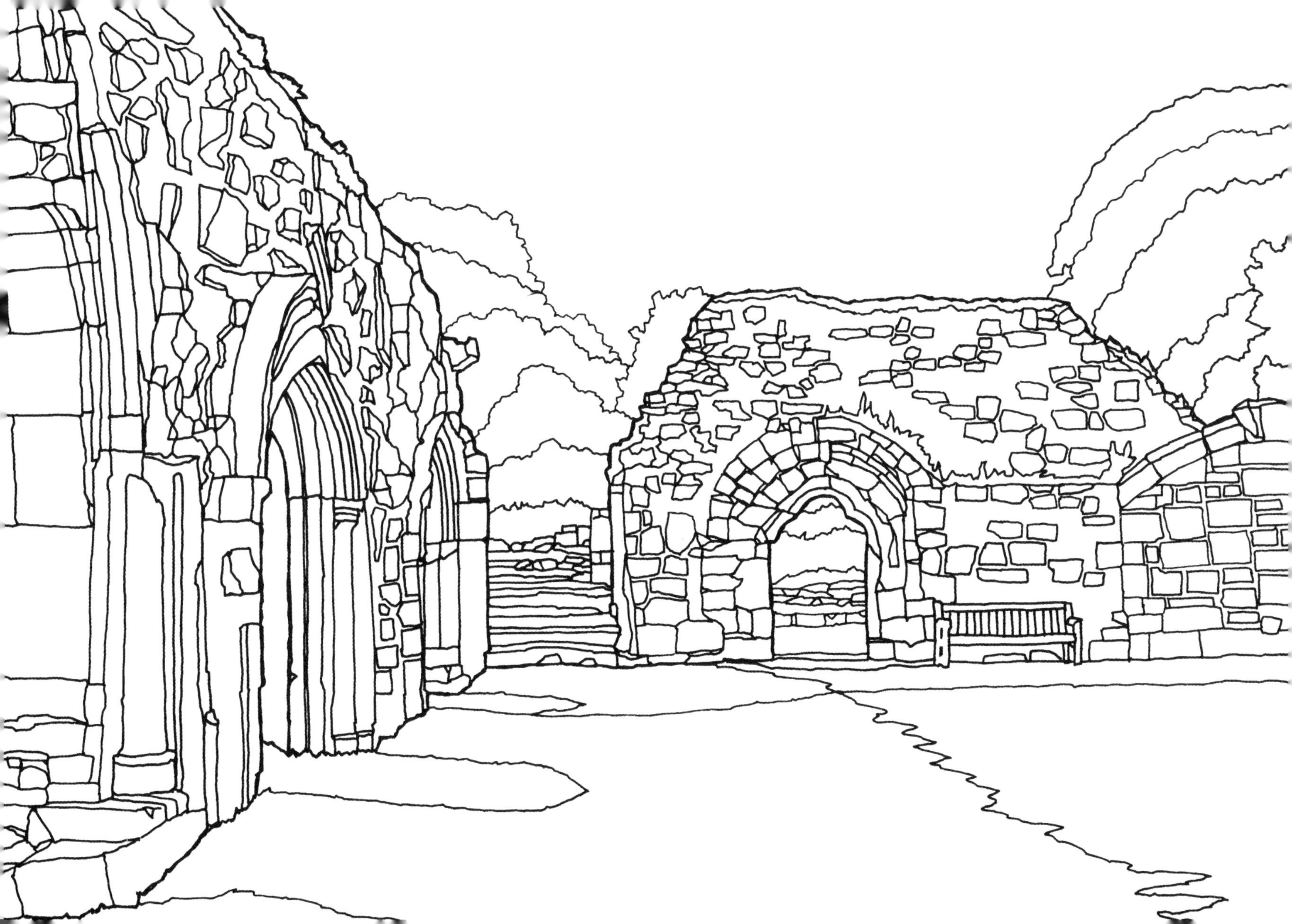

Chipping Campden, Gloucestershire ▶

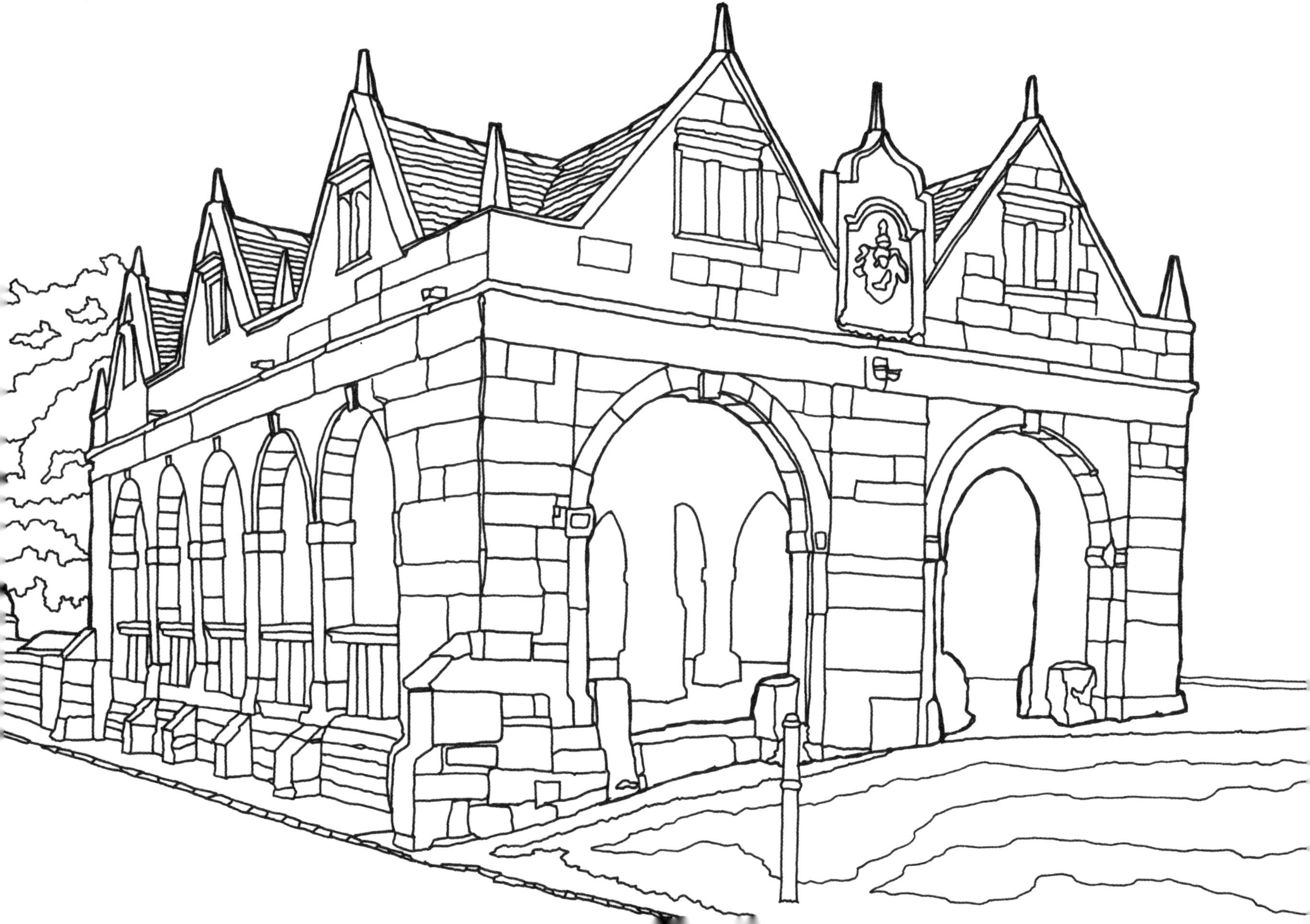

Gloucester Old Spot boar and piglet ▶

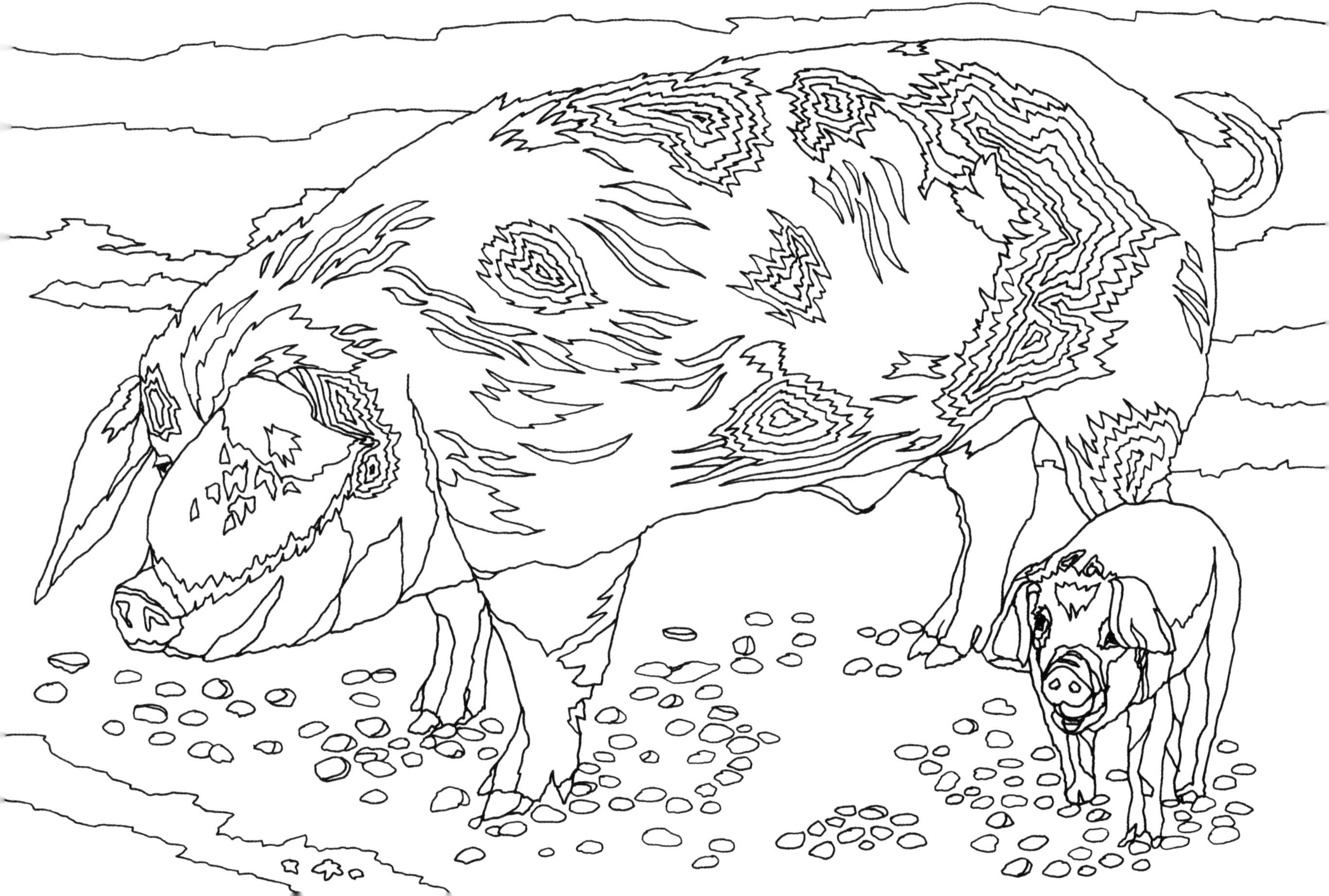

Kelmscott Manor, Oxfordshire ▶

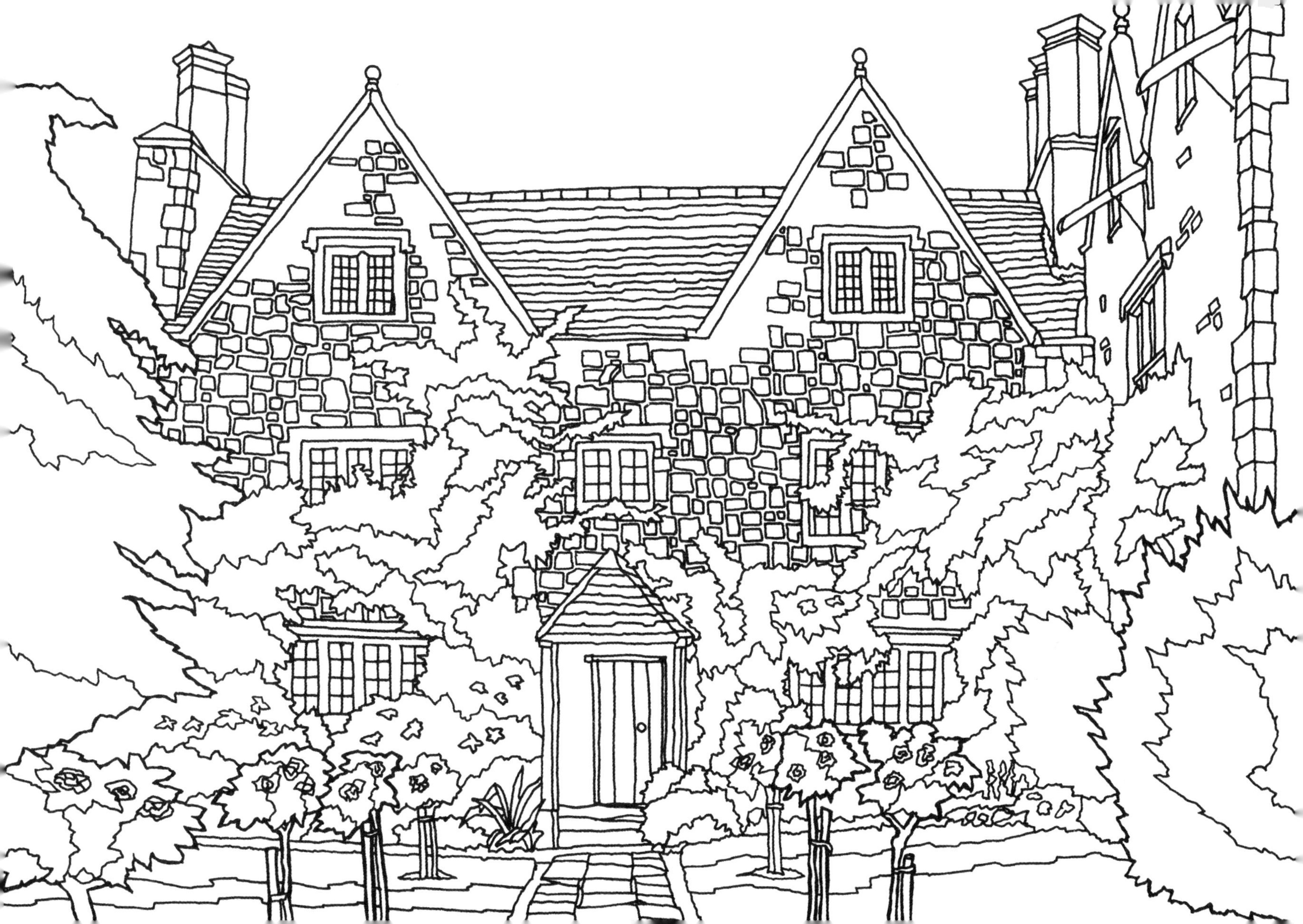

F-35 at RAF Fairford, Gloucestershire ▸

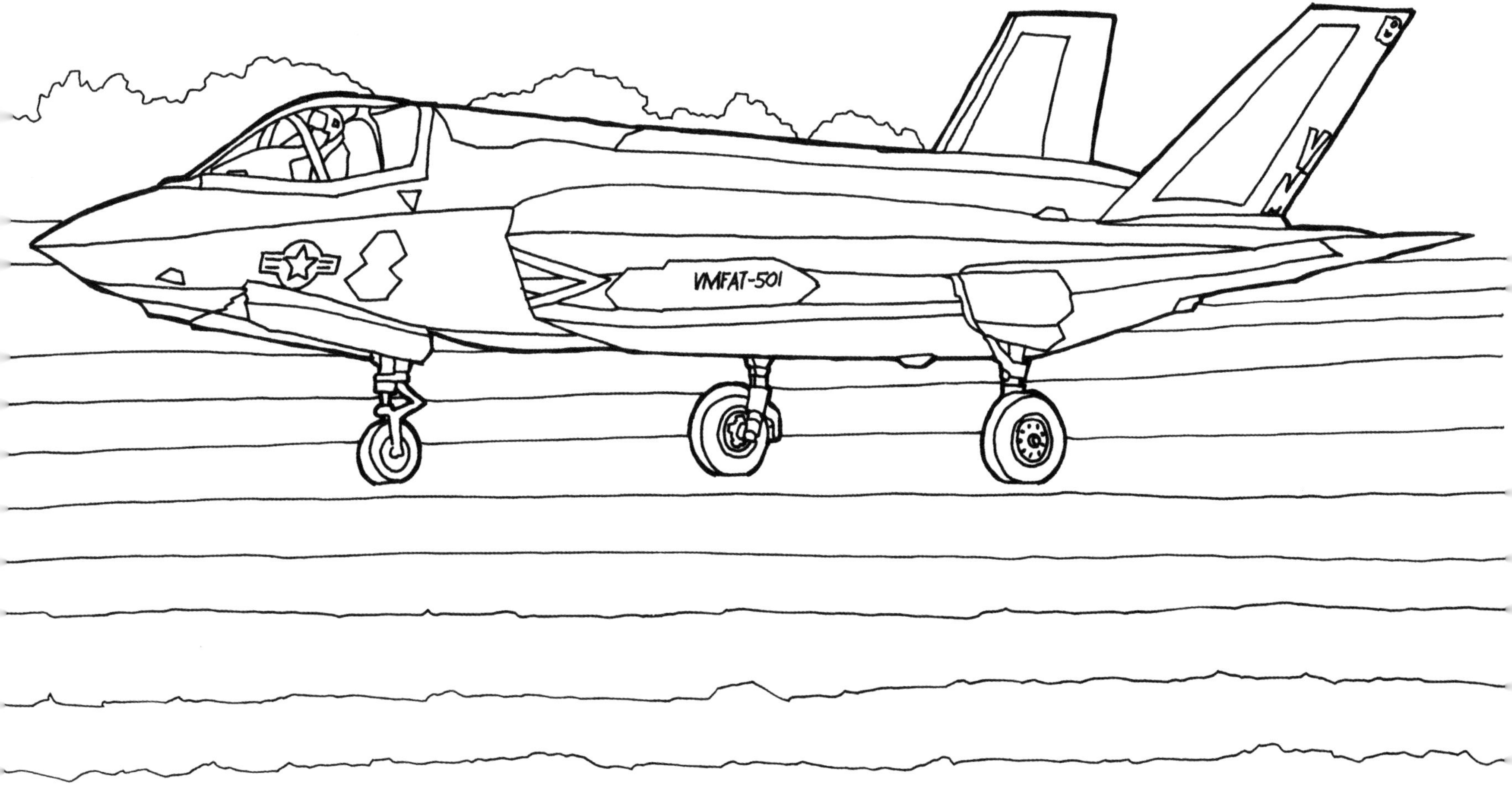
VMFAT-501

Kenilworth Castle, Warwickshire ▸

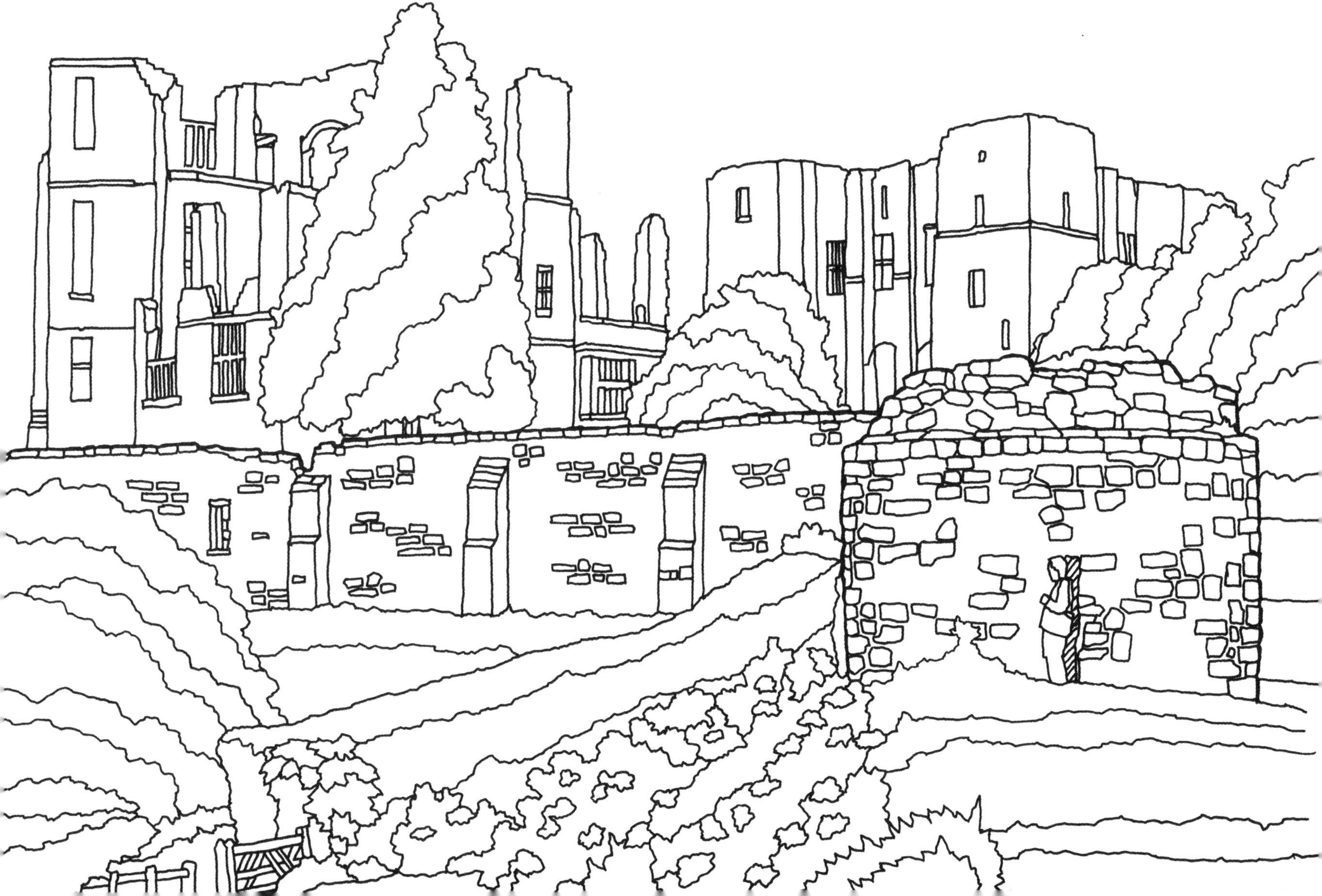

Lemur at Cotswold Wildlife Park, Oxfordshire ▶

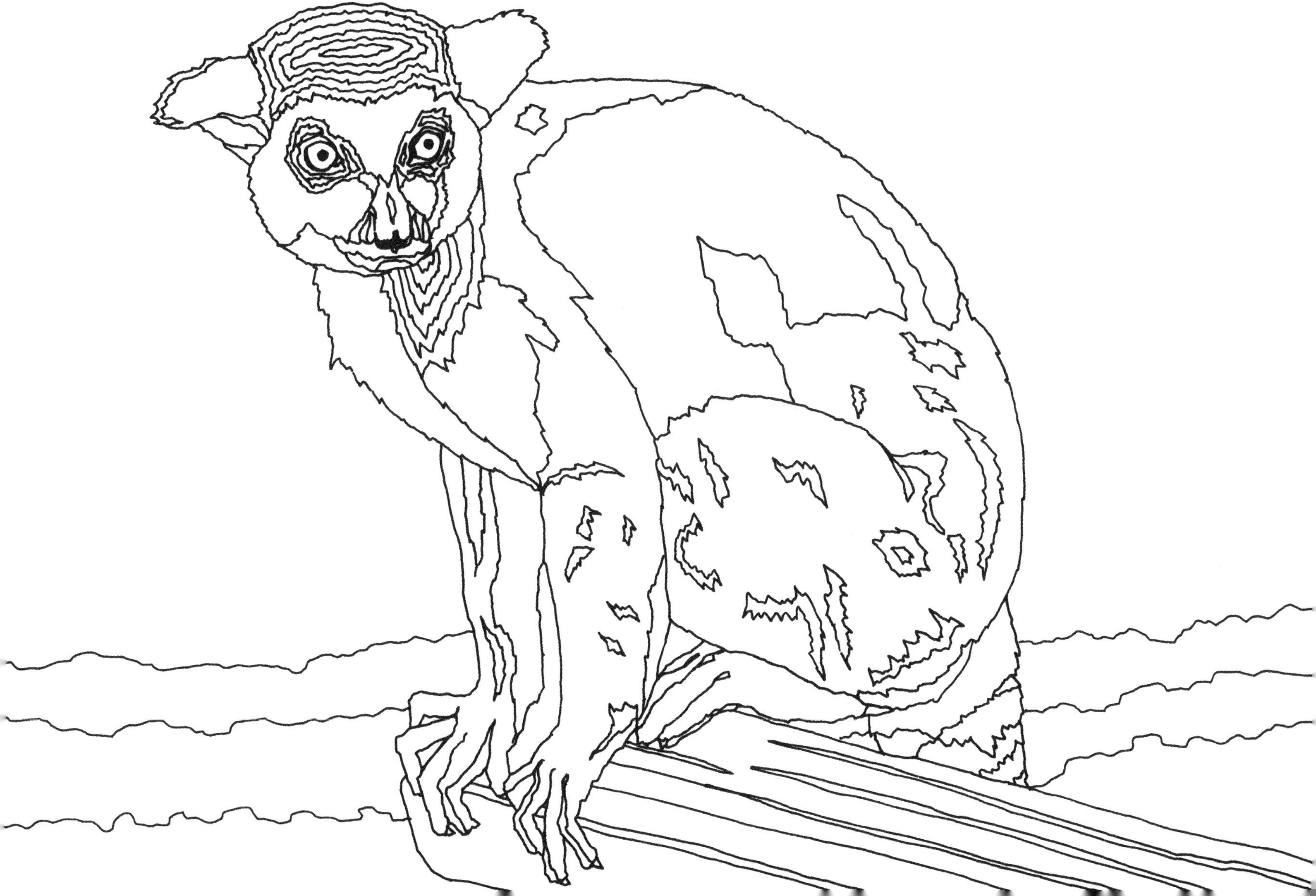

Looking up to Wotton Hill from Wotton-under-Edge, Gloucestershire, in the early twentieth century ▶

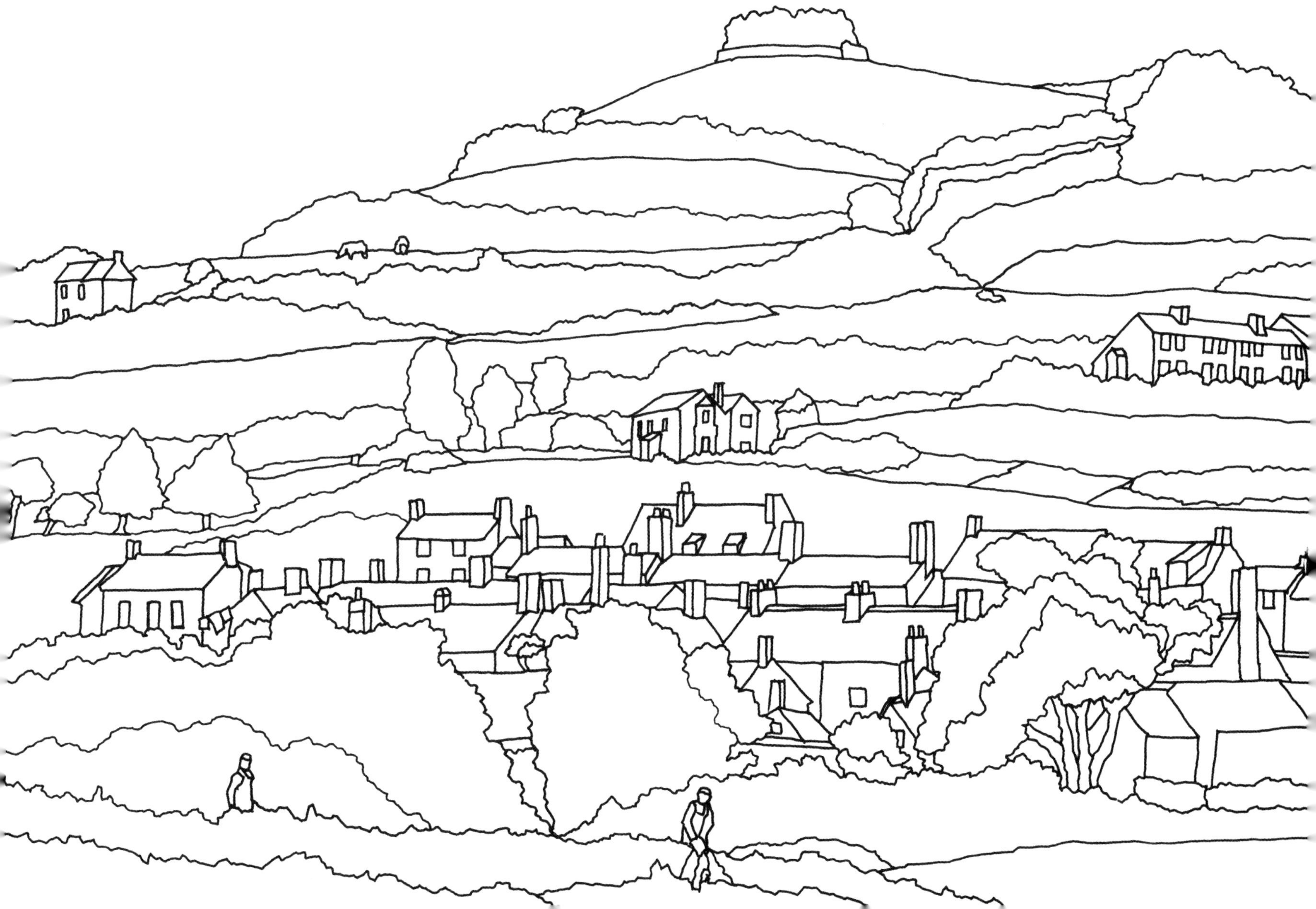

Moreton-in-Marsh, Gloucestershire ▶

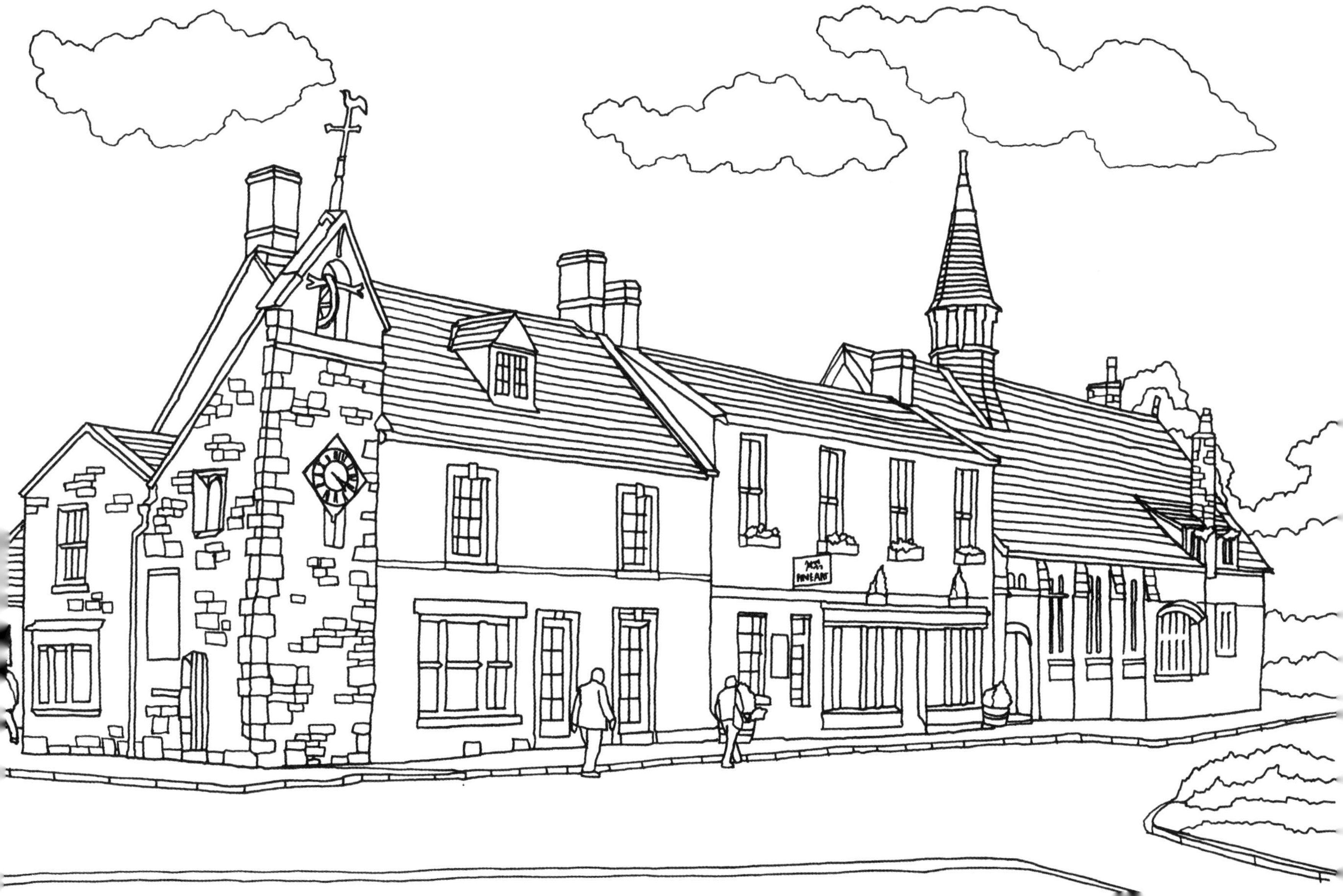

Lower Slaughter, Gloucestershire, in the 1940s ▸

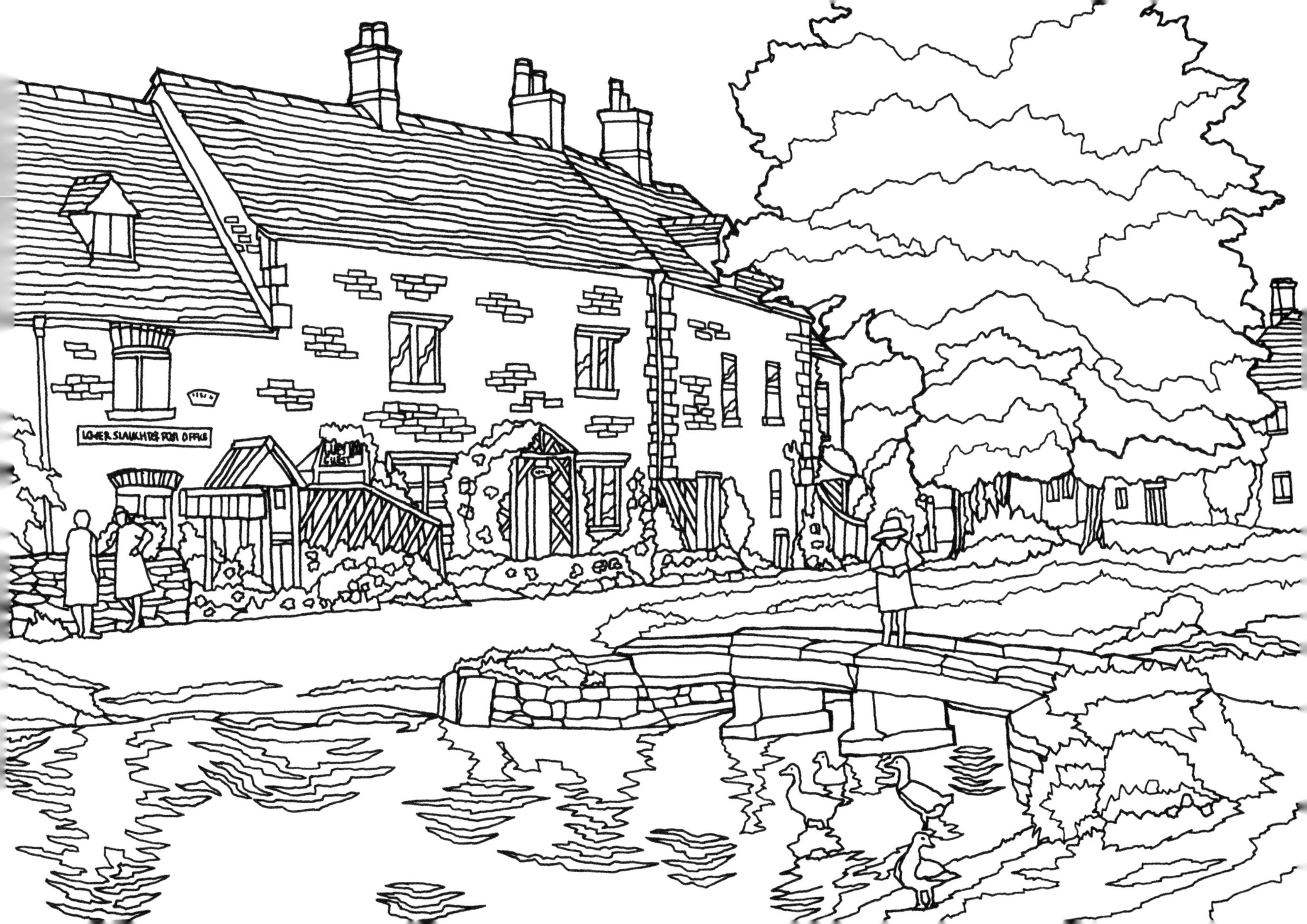
OFFICE

Chedworth Roman Villa, Gloucestershire ▶

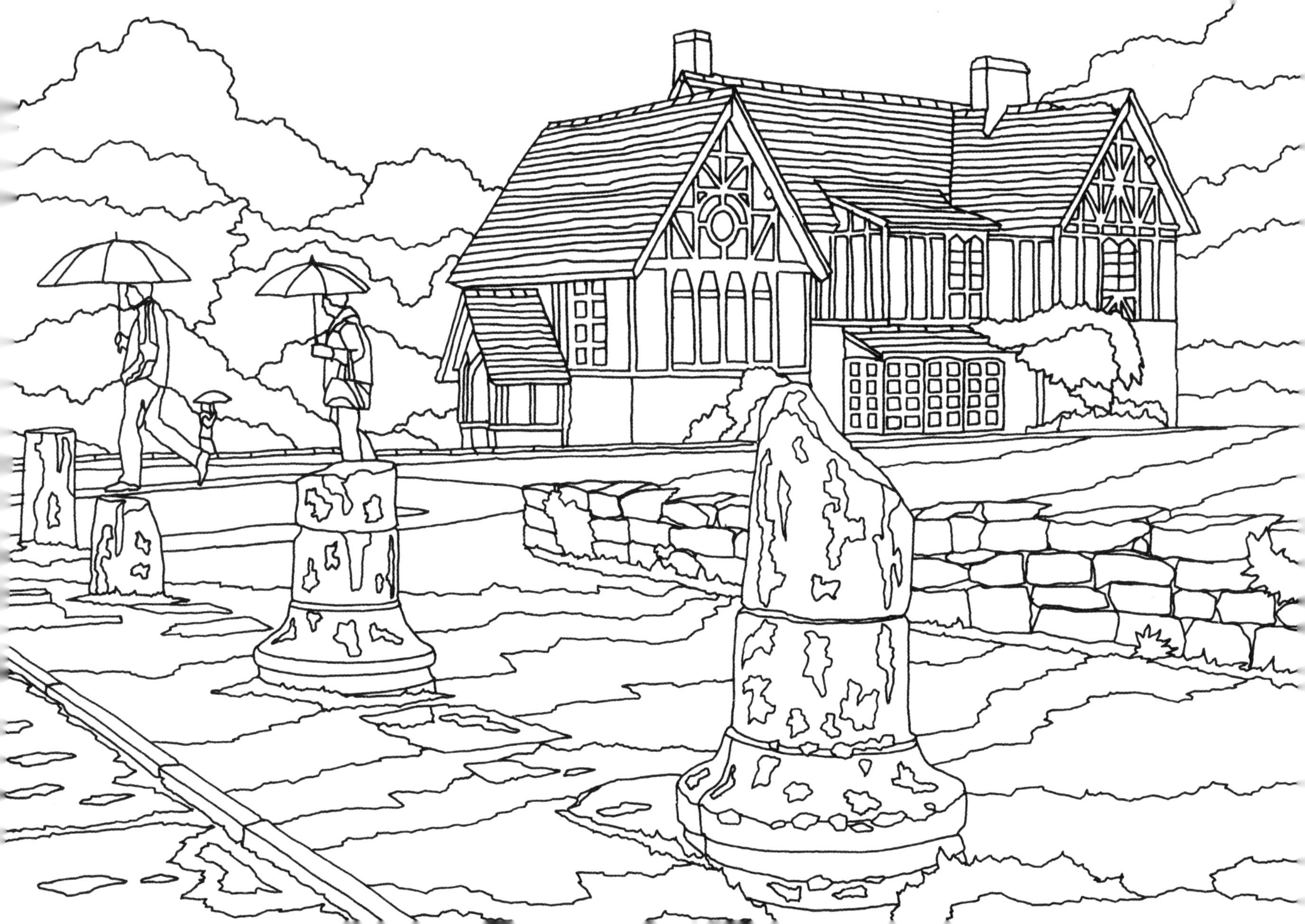

Newark Park, Gloucestershire ▸

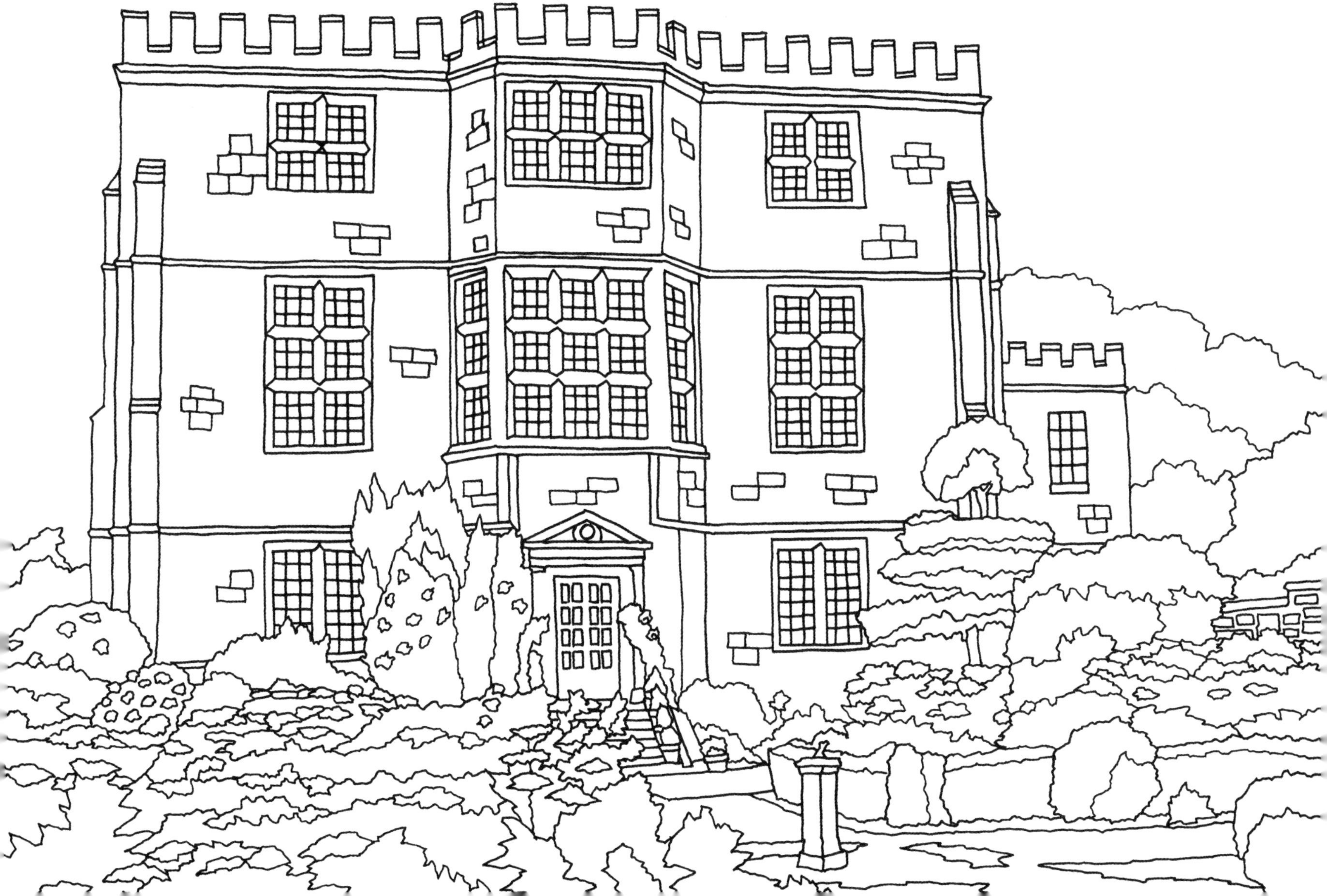

GWR (Gloucestershire Warwickshire Railway)
steam train at Cheltenham Racecourse station ▸

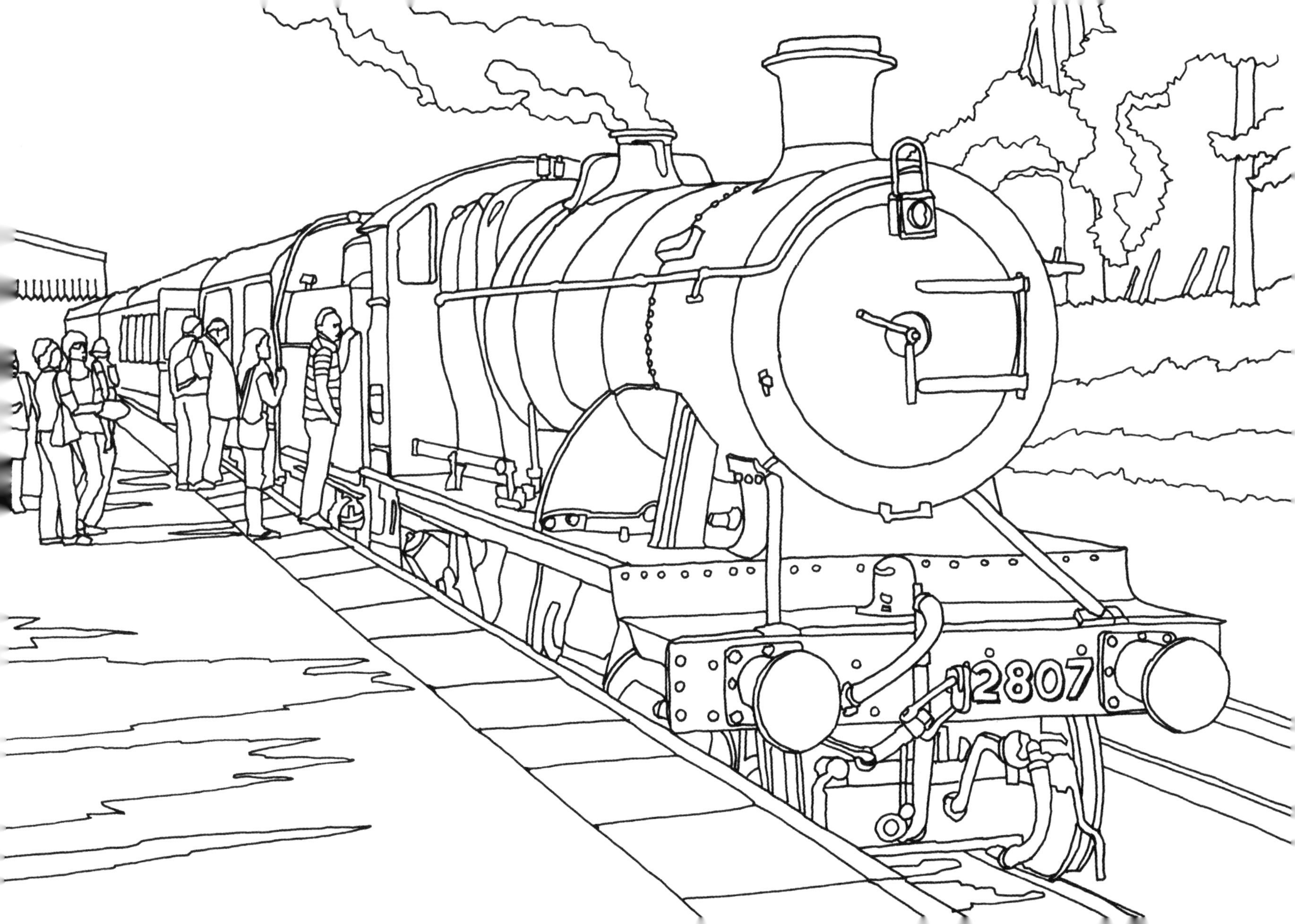
2807

Pittville Pump Room, Cheltenham, Gloucestershire ▸

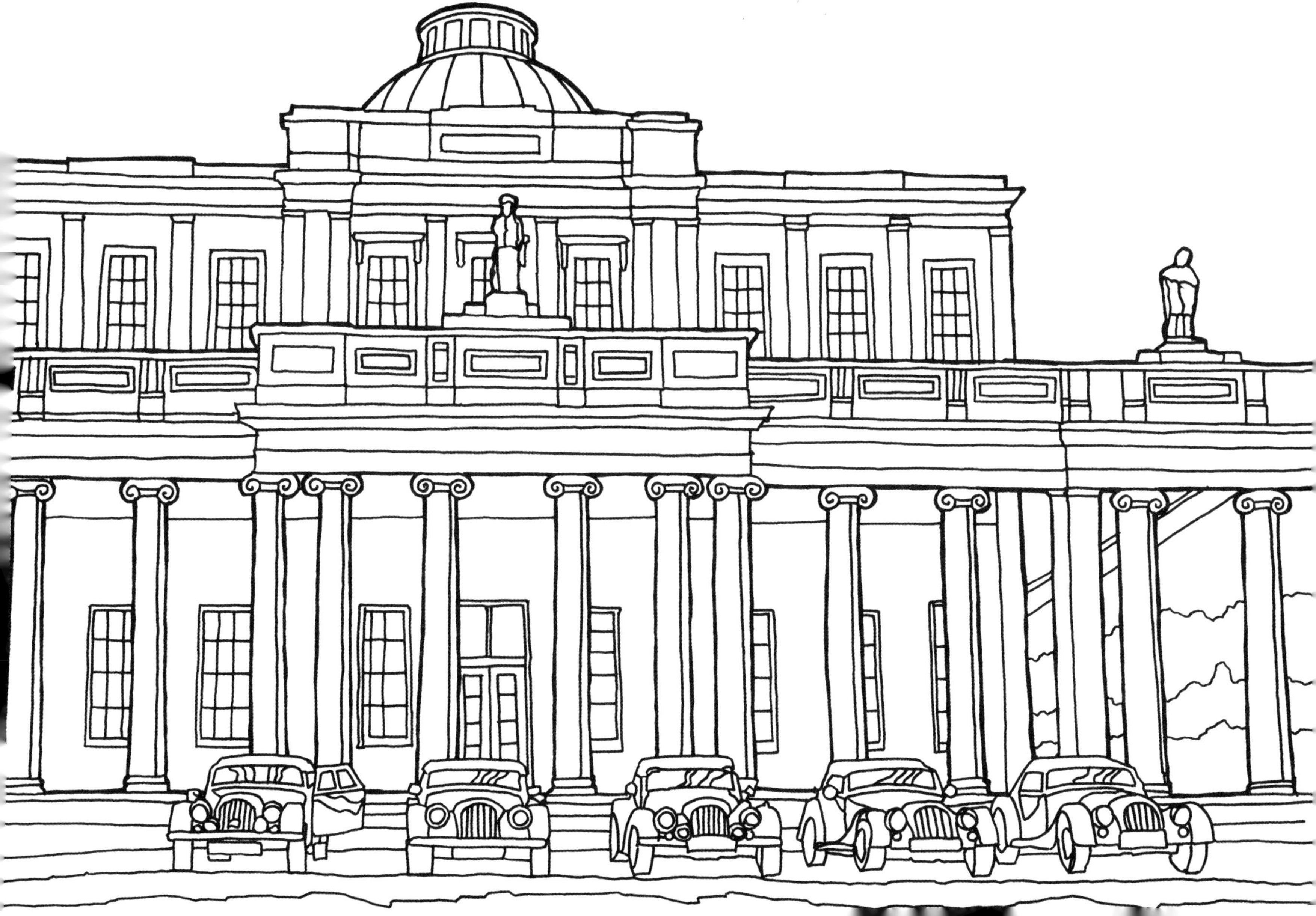

Prinknash Bird and Deer Park, Gloucestershire ▶

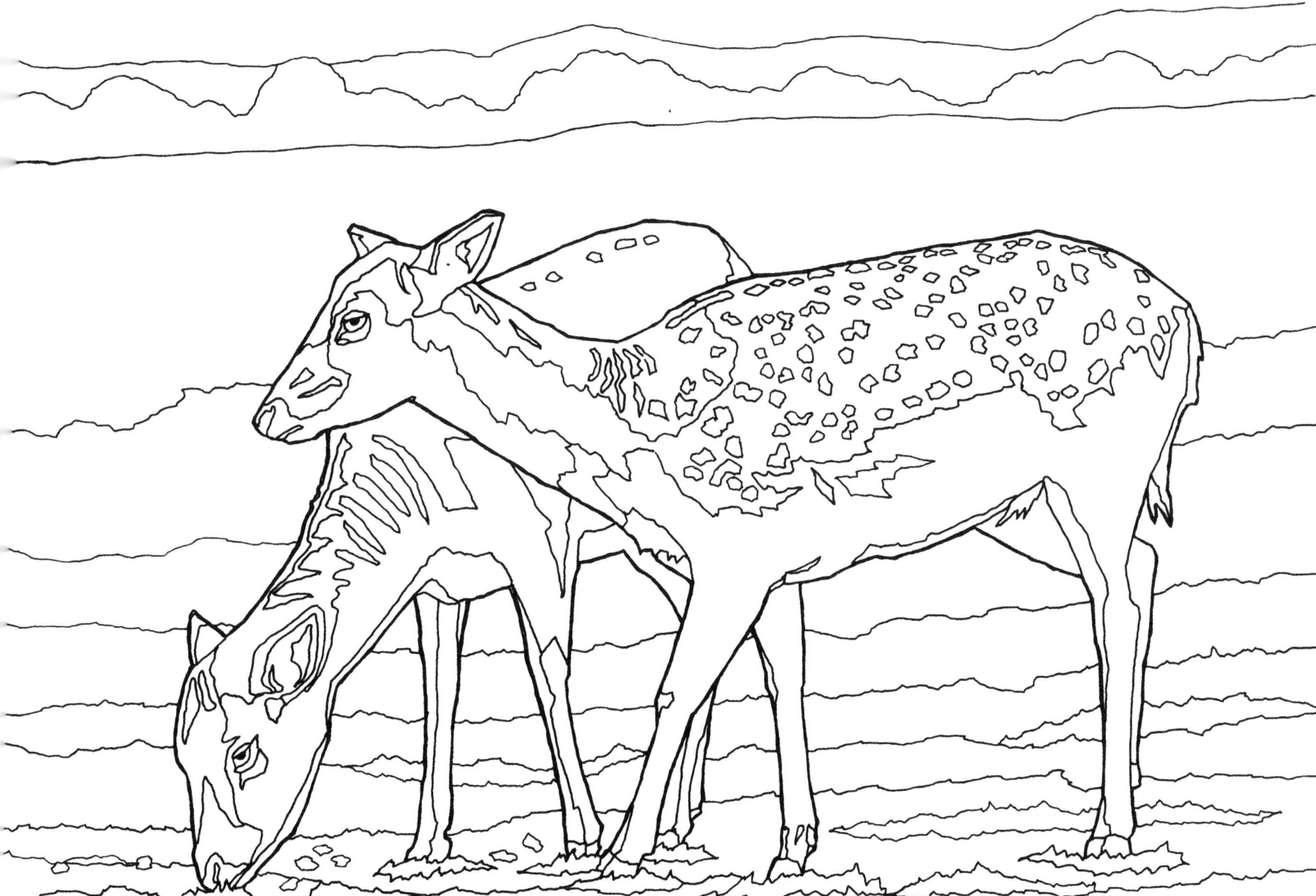

Painswick Rococo Garden, Gloucestershire ▶

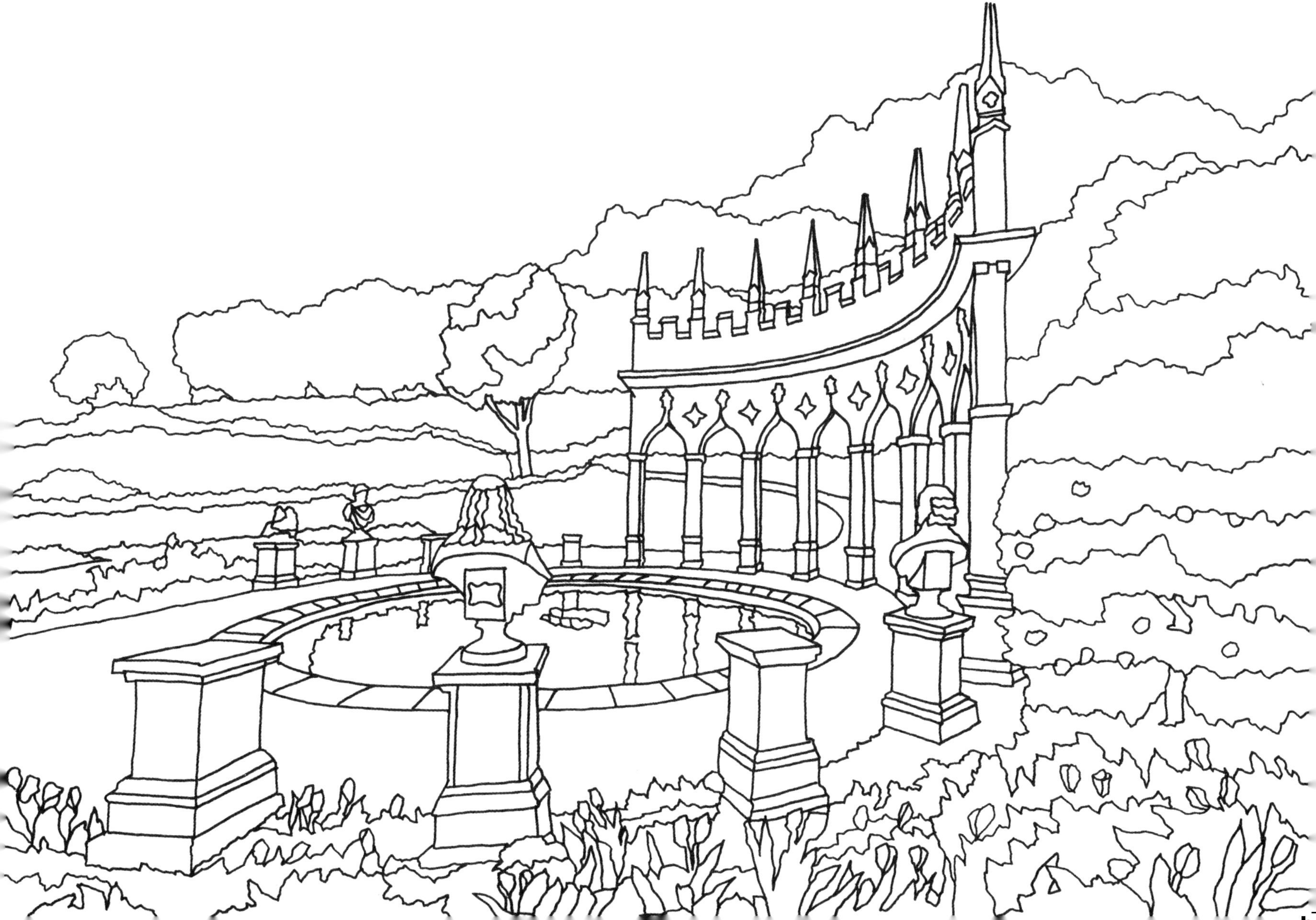

Snowshill Manor, Gloucestershire ▶

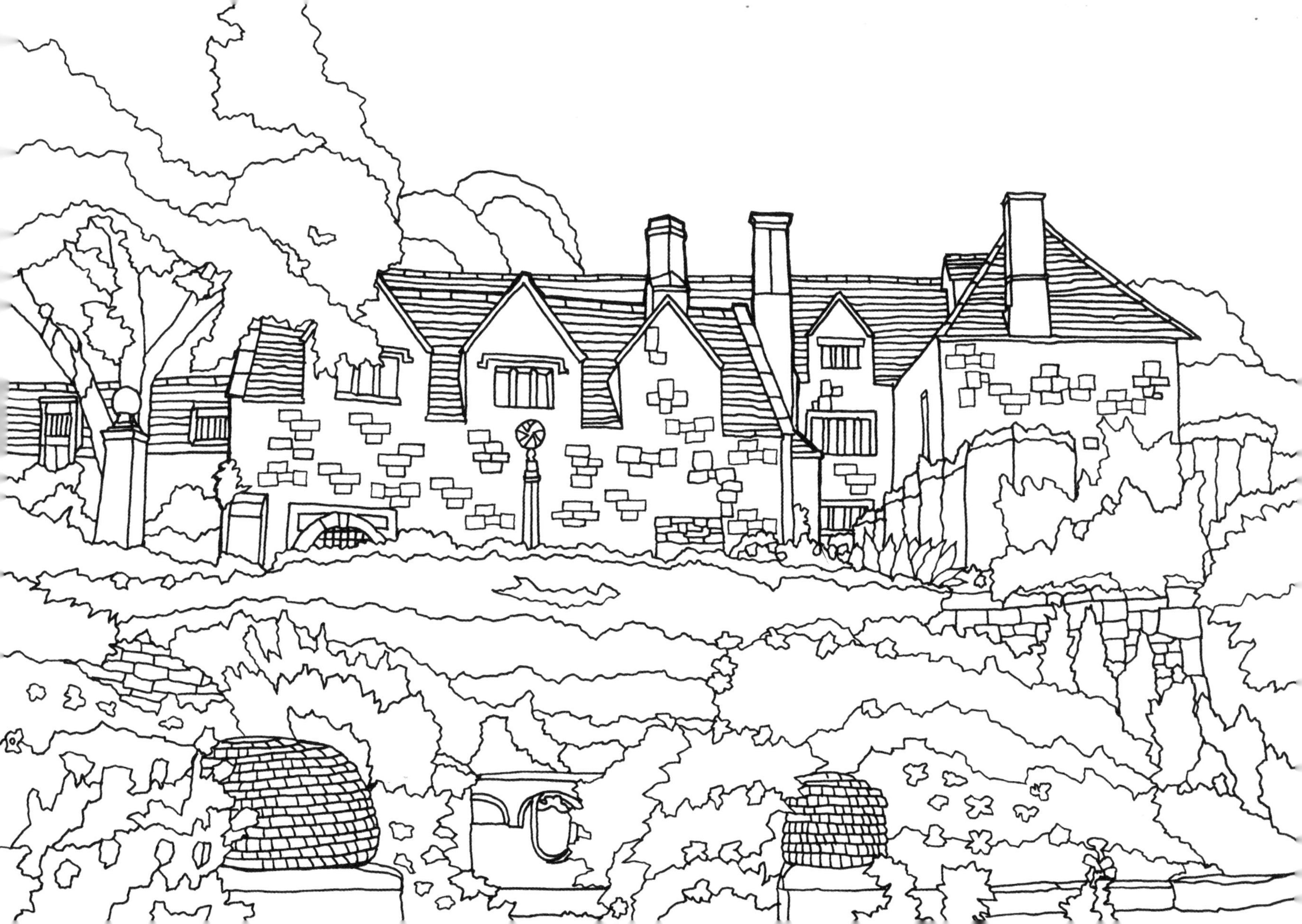

Stow-on-the-Wold, Gloucestershire ▶

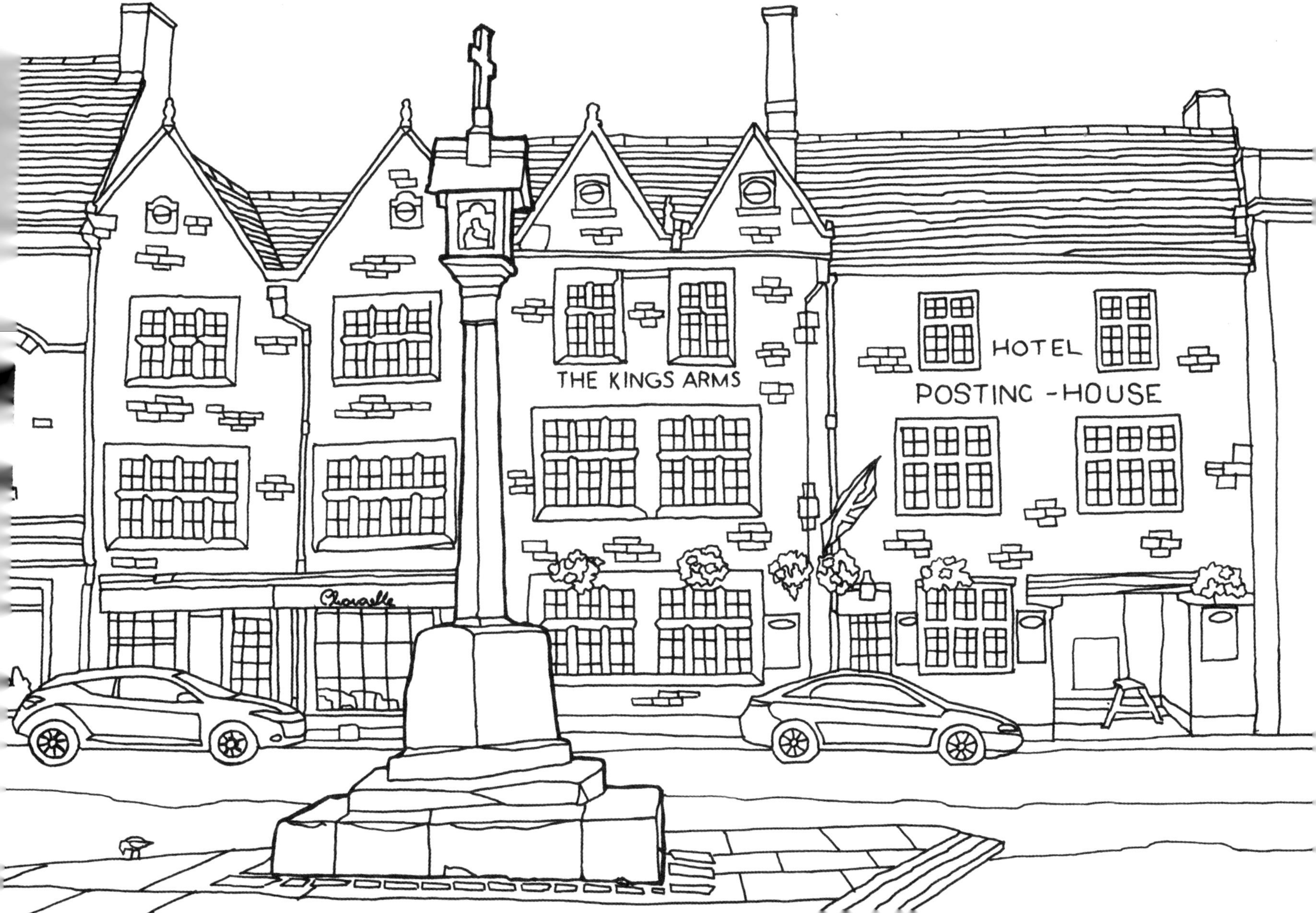
THE KINGS ARMS
HOTEL
POSTING -HOUSE

Sudeley Castle, Winchcombe, Gloucestershire ▶

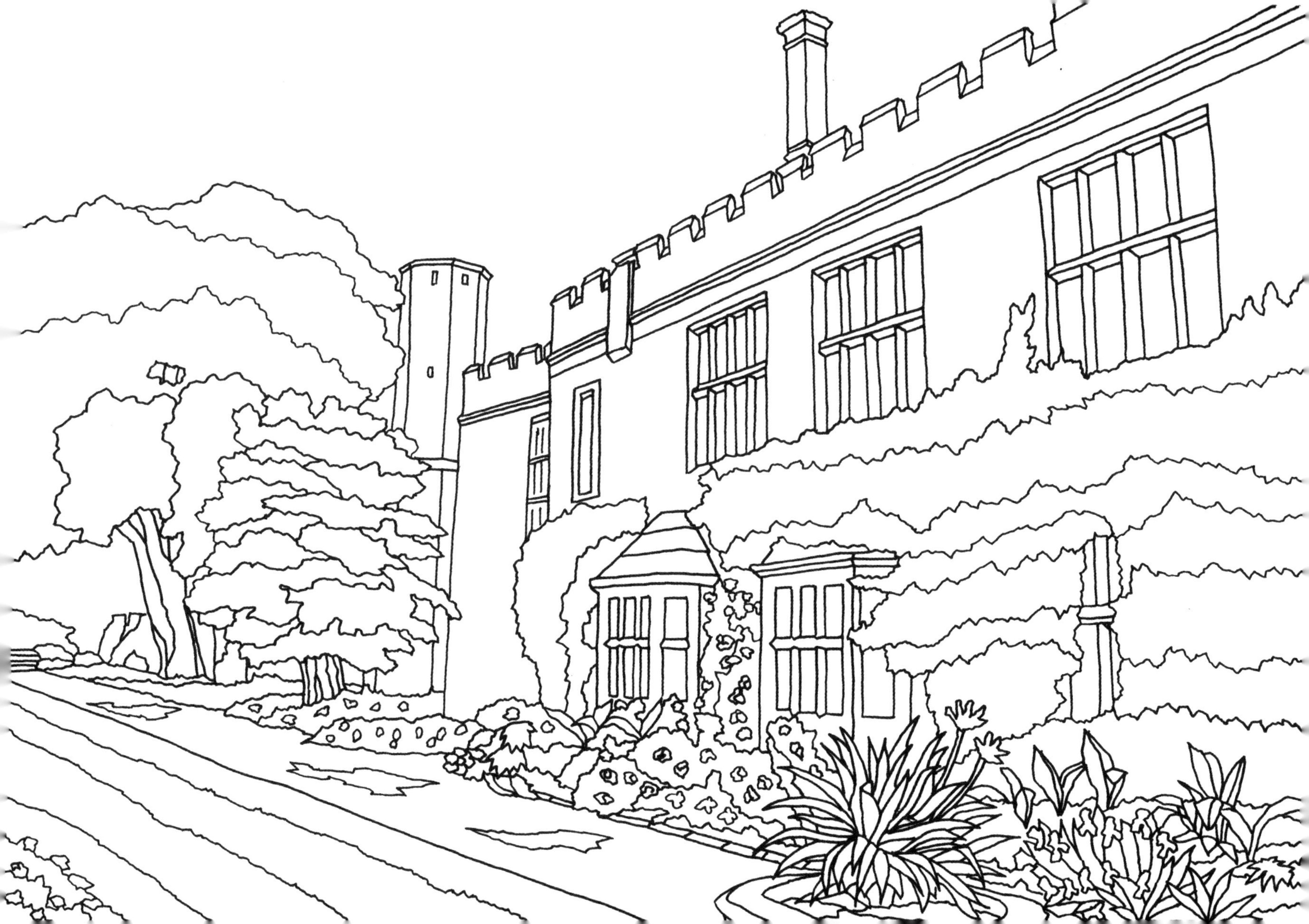

Tewkesbury Abbey, Gloucestershire ▶

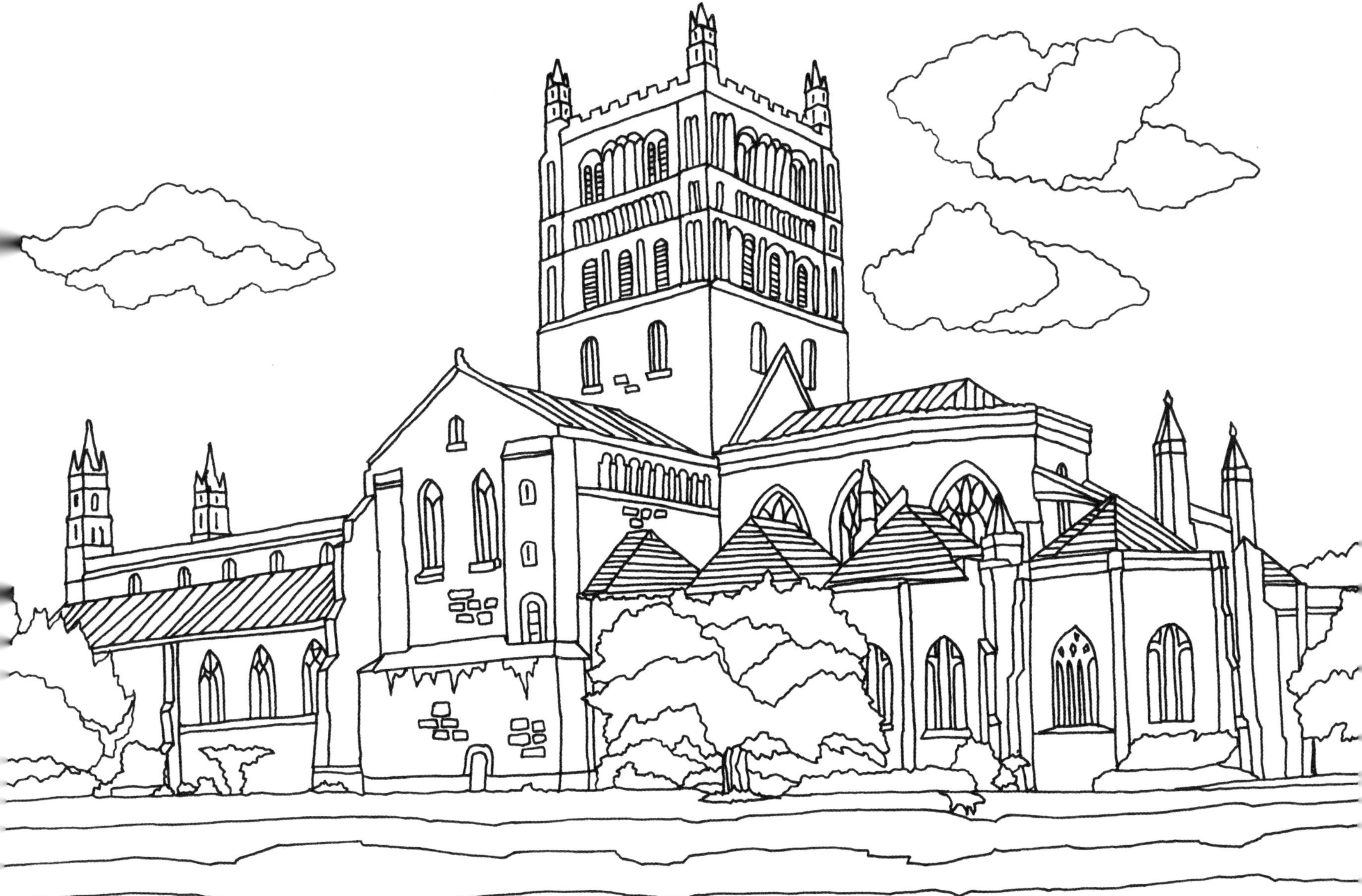

Westonbirt Arboretum, Gloucestershire ▶

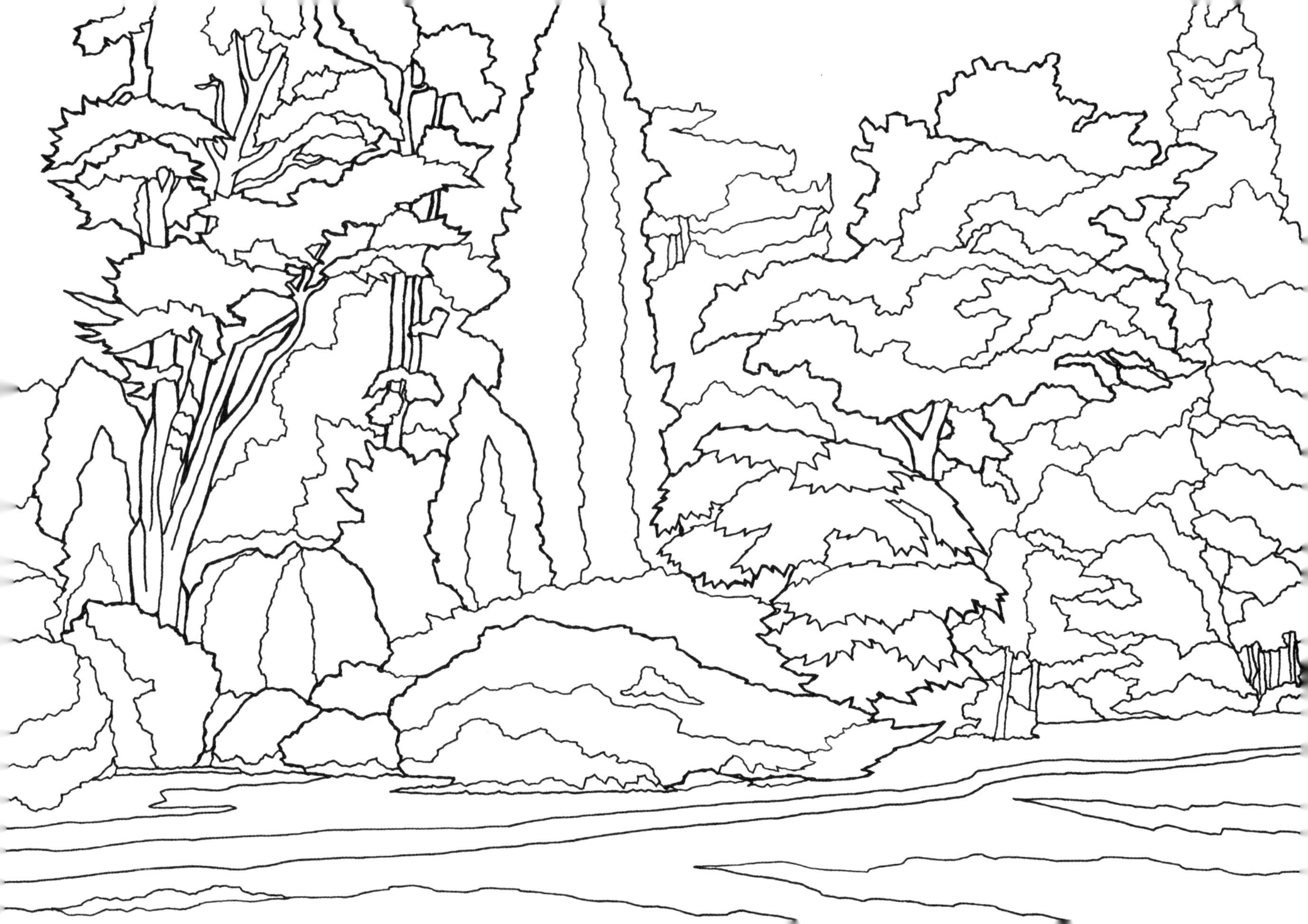

Castle Combe, Wiltshire ▶

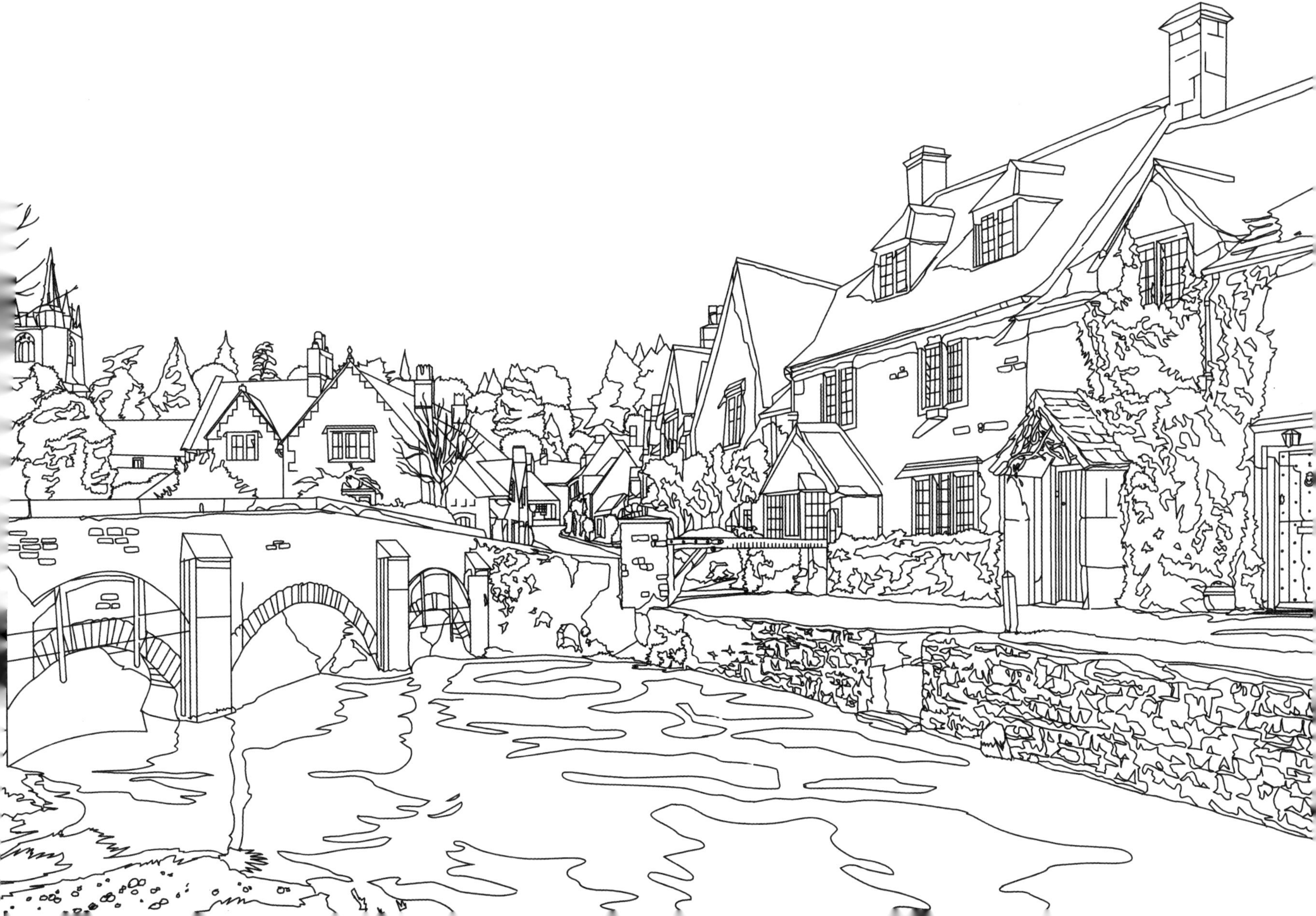

Also from The History Press

THE OXFORDSHIRE
COLOURING BOOK

PAST AND PRESENT

Find this colouring book and more at
www.thehistorypress.co.uk